A Voice in the Wilderness, volume 7

Mud and Heroes

Dalen Garris

This is a work of history. Historical individuals and places and events are mentioned.

Copyright © 2021 by Dalen Garris

Published by Revivalfire Ministries
Cover design by Kevin Haislip

ISBN 13: 978-1-7342213-7-4

All rights reserved.
No part of this book may be used or reproduced in any manner whatsoever, without written permission, except in the case of brief quotations embodied in critical articles and reviews, as provided by U.S. Copyright Law.

All Scripture is from the King James Version

For information, address
dale@revivalfire.org

First paperback printing May, 2021

Printed in the United States of America

Dedication

Willie Nelson's heroes may have always been cowboys, but mine have been the guys who went into dark places to shine bright lights. Folk heroes and mavericks have a dusty, rebellious charm to them, but the kind of heroes that I follow don't have that same appeal. They go into dangerous places with an unpopular message that gives rise to persecution instead of praise, armed with nothing but faith as their shield of courage.

The Old Testament prophets were watchmen on the wall who had unctions from God to go into difficult places and drop God's word of warning. There are others, however, who go beyond that to not only bring the warning but continue to stand in the gaps with an unpopular gospel and press the message forward until repentance comes and a move of God breaks out. These are my heroes.

There are a few names that we all know – Finney, Billy Sunday, Amy McPherson, Steve Hill – but most of them usually remain unsung heroes. Nobody knows who they are. And that is what makes it even more heroic to me. They took an unpopular message about righteousness and judgment for little or no reward and rose from lowly beginnings to shine the Light in the Dark.

They are heroes that come with nothing but God's vision driving them to turn darkness into light, death into life, and apostasy into a true Holy Ghost revival. Simple heroes from humble beginnings. Common people with uncommon zeal and no ambition to be anything more than to be an effective witness for the Lord.

Abraham confessed that he was merely "dust and ashes" – dust from the mud and ashes from the fire. Mud and heroes.

It's to those heroes that I honor and dedicate this book.

Table of Contents

Dedication	iii
Mud and Heroes	1
Oxen	3
Casting Dust	6
Sure	9
Cost	12
A Fool Rageth	15
Lamentations – Something Lost	18
Going Home	20
The Christmas Nail	22
The Esther Church	24
Mary at Christmas	27
Abraham and Abimelech	29
Nathan	32
Passing on the Glory	34
Puritans	36
The Substance of Faith	38
Timex	41
Where's the Line?	43
Amazed	46
Her candle goeth not out by night.	49
Solomon's Love Affair	51
Lazarus	54
Whole Duty of Man	57
Retail Store	60
Virgin	63
20 Minutes	66
The Zeal of Youth	69

Charity	**71**
An Abundance of Rain	**74**
Sugar Cane	**77**
Small Places	**80**
Wine and Lees	**84**
A Sound in the Mulberry Trees	**87**
Child Bearing	**90**
Crucified Walk Through Suffering	**93**
Three Types of People	**96**
Eagles	**98**
EULA	**101**
Neighborhoods	**104**
By the Brook Cherith	**108**
Three Wise Women	**112**
They Sang	**114**
70 Virgins	**117**
Car Salesmen	**120**
Mary	**123**
Subjection.	**126**
Stampede	**129**
Untempered Mortar	**133**
Welsh Revival	**136**
About the Author	**139**

Mud and Heroes

Last night, I had a T-bone steak for dinner. As I sat in a restaurant in Nairobi enjoying one of the few good meals I have had in the last month or so, I thought about how many people here have no idea what it is like to have the type of dinner I was eating and never will.

Here in Kenya, it is hard not to write about the poverty and the desperate conditions because you're engulfed in it throughout the whole country. Nairobi seems worse because of the concentration of people, but it isn't any better out in the countryside or in other cities in Kenya.

There is a section of the society that is prosperous, but I have not spent much time in that part of Nairobi and have seen very little of it. The gap between them and the overwhelming bulk of people is wide. Prices for most consumer items are comparable to the U.S., but few people can afford them because most people make about $5.00 a day if they can get a job.

There is some insidious relation between mud and poverty, as if they were cousins in human oppression. Mud mingled with trash is everywhere, and it coats every part of their existence. When the mud is gone, it is replaced by a coating of dust that digs into your spirit, weighing it down into the dirt.

Poverty is so ubiquitous that people have become oblivious to the conditions around them. And yet, these conditions not only do not stop these people but seem to cause heroes to rise out of the midst of them. I met one such hero the other day.

I was speaking at a meeting of local pastors, and at the end of the meeting, a man stood up to ask for prayer. He was dressed in shabby clothing, and it was obvious that he had little, if anything, in his pockets. He was about to head into an extremely difficult area to evangelize it and asked for the prayers of the pastors assembled there. He would be facing challenges there that Americans are not able to grasp. He would be going in there alone with no resources, no friends, and no support.

I quickly offered him a whole case of Bibles to take with him, and as I held hands with him and prayed, the Lord showed me the dark and difficult path this man was about to enter. It was so dark and heavy that I shuddered.

I asked him if he was aware of what I was seeing, and his answer came back quickly and crisply. Yes, he knew. Period. That was it. He knew. There were no other considerations for him to pause over, ponder, or worry about – he simply knew how hard it was going to be, and that was that.

I watched as he strode down that muddy street, a case of Bibles hoisted on his shoulder, with little more than the thousand shilling note I gave him in his pocket, heading off to a greater challenge than most of us will ever face in our whole lives. There was something about the way he was walking down that street that got to me. He wasn't walking – he was marching.

I will probably never see that man again, but someday we will meet on the other side. I will ask him to sit down and tell me the story of the battles that he went off to face, armed with nothing but a confident faith in God, a serious dedication to the mission before him, and a case of Bibles.

Today was a good day. I watched a genuine hero march off to war.

Oxen

Where no oxen are, the crib is clean: but much increase is by the strength of the ox.

(Proverbs 14:4)

Work. Ugh! Don't you just hate it?

You cannot escape work. We try all sorts of ways to get around it, but we never escape it. It is one of the "blessings" that came out of the Garden of Eden, and it has dogged our tracks ever since.

It is no different with the church.

Oxen are dirty animals. You have to clean them, feed them, and even build a crib for them to stay in. And good luck trying to potty-train them. Guess who has to shovel up all the stuff that they leave you.

There is a way to escape all that work, however – get rid of the oxen. That way, the crib stays clean, and you can relax, which is what you wanted in the first place, right? Relax and cruise through life. Ahh, the peaceful life!

But if you want an increase, if you want your crops to grow, and if you want to eat, then you need those oxen to pull the plow, and that means work.

No church will ever grow without the strength of its pastor. He is the ox that pulls the plow. If your ox is weak and lethargic, you won't get much plowing done. If the ox is taken up with other things that are much more fascinating than those boring, straight rows of dirt, you will end up with crooked rows that run in every direction other than the one you need to get the field done. No, the ox has to work and work hard; otherwise, there will be no harvest.

But just having oxen doesn't constitute a harvest. You can't just stick him in the crib, go back to relax on the porch, and expect bushels of wheat to drop out of the sky. Sorry, it doesn't work like that. You have to put your hand to the plow and get out there and work with him.

I hear so many Christians complain about how hard it is to find a good church. They complain that wherever they go, services are dead, and they feel like they are just going through the motions. They are hard-pressed to find a soul-winning church where the power of the Spirit of God can be felt rather than mimicked.

And forget about miracles of healing and prayer! Instead of the power of God, all they find are carnal celebrations to pump up emotional highs. It feels good, and it's lots of fun, but it's not what they are looking for. They want the real thing. We used to have it, but we lost it somewhere along the line.

And so, we blame the churches and their pastors for what we feel is missing. "Woe to the pastors that scatter the flocks," we say. We complain that the oxen don't have the strength and the drive to do the work. True, a weak message will not produce a strong congregation, but aren't we still just trying to get out of that work? If we want a strong church, then we must have a strong ox, but when you get a strong ox, that means you will have to get out there in the field and work as hard as the ox does.

Oops.

Isn't there an easier way? Can't we just get the oxen to do all the work while we sit back and enjoy the benefits of a strong, powerful church? Can't we just hitch the oxen up to the plow and let them run around the field by themselves?

No, you must put your hand to the plow. The plow has two handles -- you put your hand on one handle while God puts his hand on the other handle, and you drive those oxen in a straight line if you want your crops to grow.

And who goes out there after the field is plowed to plant the seed? Not the oxen – they're back in the crib. And who does the weeding? And the watering? And the reaping? Is Jesus supposed to do all that for you? Jesus said that He would separate the wheat from the chaff, but you have to bring the harvest into the threshing floor so He can do that.

The oxen will work if you work them. People who want a strong, soul-winning church will gravitate to a pastor who delivers a strong message, but a strong ox cannot do it alone. It is up to you to work the plow.

Don't complain about the pastor if you're not willing to clean the crib.

And Jesus said unto him, No man, having put his hand to the plough, and looking back, is fit for the kingdom of God.

(Luke 9:62)

Casting Dust

> *"And they gave him audience unto this word, then lifted up their voices, and said, 'Away with such a fellow from the earth: for it is not fit that he should live.'*
>
> *And as they cried out, and cast off their clothes, and threw dust into the air, the chief captain commanded him [Paul] to be brought into the castle...."*
>
> *(Acts 22:22-24)*

What a picture that must have been! I can just see these guys running around crazy, throwing up clouds of dirt in the air while they're ripping off their clothes. And after all was said and done, they were left dirty, naked, and cold. And no Paul.

Yeah, that worked great, didn't it?

Some of you parents out there are familiar with scenes like this with your children, aren't you? But these were adults throwing temper tantrums, not children. And, as if that wasn't enough, a bunch of these guys, not satisfied with their little display, decided to bind themselves with a great curse that they would not eat or drink until they had killed Paul.

So, how'd that work out for you guys?

And how'd that first mouthful of bread taste when you found out that your plan had failed? Not much of a choice you've left yourself with – either accept your own stupid curse or starve to death. What on earth were you thinking about?

Real smart boys. I sure hope their next employer asked for a resume before hiring them for anything that required more sense than sweeping up the dirt they just threw all over the place. I can see it all now – "Yes, sir. We sure showed them! We threw all that dirt in the air and ran around naked. That'll teach those Christians!" That is, of course, if any of you were left after your nice, long fast.

What is the deal with some people? Is it something in the water they've been drinking, or is it just a case of really bad genetics? Were they born that stupid, or did they learn it over time?

There is something about religious fervor that defies common sense. I may not agree with your politics, but I'm not going to go beat you up over it. I'm a die-hard New York Yankees fan, but I'm not going to shoot somebody just because they root for the Boston Red Sox. But oh boy, get into the arena of religion, and suddenly, the issue takes on an insane intensity.

And it's not usually with non-believers, but with those who are stuck on some form of religion, whether it be Christianity, Muslim, Hindu, or even Communism and Fascism (which is just a form of religion in political clothing).

But that intense hatred is not borne by true Christians.

True Christians have been the target of persecution since Jesus Christ was nailed to the Cross, and it is still going on today in many places around the world. Now, I'm not talking about the Crusades or wars fought in the name of Christ, but about real Christians who have carried the message of Salvation to a lost and dying world and have been rewarded for their efforts with imprisonment, torture, and death.

What is it about the Gospel of Jesus Christ that is such a threat that drives these zealots crazy – crazy enough to kill Jesus Christ Himself?

The nearest I can figure is that this is war, and Satan knows the threat of Christ's message to his satanic kingdom. It exposes the cheap imitations he has sold to humanity and sheds light on the darkness he has blanketed the world with. He has no morals and no soft, warm, fuzzy spot in his blackened heart, so he will send those whom he can control on a rampage to stop the Gospel at any cost.

The problem is not that we are at war -- it's that too many Christians don't realize it.

Sure

I think religious fervor can be insane (or at least can lead to insanity), but there is also much to be said for standing your ground for your beliefs. Too many of us are willing to compromise our bedrock beliefs in the interest of communal peace. That's great for making friends but can have an eroding effect on our integrity before God. But how can we know with complete certainty that what we have based our faith on is right?

There is no other issue as important as the destiny of our eternal souls and how we plan on getting there, but first, we need to be sure of what our faith is based on; otherwise, we will have nothing more than a cacophony of meddling voices that make no sense and have little effect.

I want to <u>know</u> I am saved, not <u>guess</u>. I want positive, rock-solid evidence that I am right with God -- not based on what I know, what I think I know, or what sounds like a good idea. I don't want a faith that is based solely on what I have been told by my mother or some spiritual philosophies that I have heard. I want to be so sure of my salvation that the power of God stands every day as ever-present evidence in my life -- not something that happened to me once upon a time, but today, as I am breathing right now.

I want to be so sure that I would give my life for it.

Peter said, "And we believe and are sure that thou art that Christ, the Son of the living God" (John 6:69). What made Peter so sure Christ was the Son of God that he was willing to follow his Savior to the cross?

David spoke in Psalm 91:1 of dwelling in the "secret place of the Most High" where he would know beyond any doubt that the promises of God belonged to him. What is this secret place that you can dwell in that is so different from the world that, even in the face of sure destruction, you can rest in the knowledge that you are abiding under the shadow of the Almighty?

I want to <u>know</u> I am saved, and I want to know now, not when I finally face the Judgment Bar of God. I can think of nothing worse than to spend my life thinking I was serving the Lord, only to find out I was wrong and have to face an eternity in Hell.

Paul said that faith is the substance of things hoped for (Heb. 11:1). There is a substance to faith that is real – you can actually feel it. He wrote that our hope is as an anchor of the soul "…both sure and steadfast that entereth into that within the veil" (Heb. 6:19). Jesus Christ is the Door (John 10:9). It was His flesh that was the veil that was torn for us so that we could reach through it to touch the Throne of God and grab hold of something that, while it may sound ethereal and other-worldly, is more real than real. There is another dimension in God you can enter, which gives you a rock-solid foundation to rest your faith on. It's called walking in the Spirit of God.

In worldly terms, we say, "Follow the money," but in the spiritual realm, it is "Follow the power." Is the power of God evident in your life? Can you feel it? Can you reach out and touch it? Does it sweep over your world? Are you a brand-new creature in Christ? Have you been changed? Is your church filled with the Power of God?

I'm talking about some powerful, knock-you-down, fill-me-up, switch-on-the-lights, plug-in-the-power, jump-up-and-down, supernatural power here, folks -- not the subdued religious funeral services that we consider so "holy." I want the Real Thing, and I don't mean Coca-Cola.

If the power of God is not a tangible reality to you, then I have to ask, how do you know that you are saved? If your faith is not based on the reality of His presence, then how would you be able to walk through the Hall of Heroes in Hebrews 11? How could you willingly give your life and the lives of your loved ones to the cause of Christ without doubt or fear? How will you be able to follow Him all the way to the Cross?

Theological debate will not establish faith; that is merely eating off the Tree of the Knowledge of Good and Evil. That fruit is "desired to make one wise," but in it are the seeds of death, for "to be carnally minded is death."

I want to eat off the Tree of Life and feel the complete transformation from this life to a life in that secret place of the Most High, to see Life through His eyes, and to feel the power that is in the Blood of Jesus Christ flowing through me and bringing forth fruit unto eternal life.

I want to KNOW I am saved.

"Wherefore the rather, brethren, give diligence to make your calling and election sure..."
(1st Peter 1:10)

Cost

> *"Or what king, going to make war against another king, sitteth not down first, and consulteth whether he be able with ten thousand to meet him that cometh against him with twenty thousand?*
>
> *Or else, while the other is yet a great way off, he sendeth an ambassage, and desireth conditions of peace.*
>
> (Luke 14:31,32)

Jesus tells us to count the cost.

Any king that rushed off to battle against an army that was twice the size of his would be considered a fool. "Cut a deal with the enemy, you idiot! Why sacrifice your men to a certain slaughter? The enemy is too strong for you, and there is no hope of winning this battle. Do the sensible thing -- surrender!"

Is this what Jesus is telling us to do? To give in to the devil when he attacks? A quick read of Deuteronomy chapter 20 tells us quite the contrary —God expects us to charge into battle even when the odds are against us and trust Him for the victory instead of fearing the circumstances.

And yet, I hear excuses all the time:

- "I would love to witness at work, but I'm afraid I'll get fired."
- "I would love to give more to the ministry, but I'm afraid I won't be able to pay my bills."
- "I would like to tell my neighbor about Jesus, but I'm afraid they will think I'm weird."
- "I would love to go into the mission field that God has called me to, but how will I support my family?"
- "I want to take a stand for the Truth, but I will lose all my friends and my social standing."

- "I would like to pray at our football games, but the ACLU will sue me."
- "After all, aren't we supposed to be responsible?"
- "Jesus did tell us to count the cost, didn't He? And sometimes the cost is just too high."
- "Sometimes discretion is the better part of valor, and we should just compromise so we can all have peace."

Yes, Jesus said to count the cost, but only so you would know how much to cast to the winds: "So likewise, whosoever he be of you that forsaketh not all that he hath, he cannot be my disciple." Luke 14:33

Proverbs says that without a vision, the people perish (Prov. 29:18), but visions are not made of what you can see – they are made of what you can believe. Heroes are not created by seeing the way things are – they are created by seeing the way things will be. David killed his Goliath with a stone from the riverbed. Daniel stopped the lions' mouths without even raising his hand. The children of Israel defeated Pharaoh by wading into the water. And the list goes on.

Victories are not won by counting the cost. They are won in spite of it. It's making a decision that you are willing to sacrifice all for the cause of Christ, and you will trust God no matter what happens. Even if everything else fails, you will not. You will stand your ground and fight for the honor of God no matter what the cost.

Many of you have sat in the complacency of compromise for years, afraid to venture forth into that which the Lord has called you to. For some of you, it is a ministry that means leaving home, wealth, and comfort. Others have been called to take a personal stand at home or at work. God has challenged some of you to release that death grip you have on your money and give it away so He can use it to win souls. Each of us has that beckoning to leave our place of safety, step out into the unknown, throw caution to the winds, and proclaim that we are warriors for God and will fulfill our calling no matter what the cost!

God will give you a certain space of time to step out in faith and hold up the Blood-Stained Banner in the battle that He has set before you. Some of you will trust God and charge forth into victory, while others will shrink back into the comfortable, dark cave they have been hiding in for years, but all of us will face a decision that has to be made. Either we trust God, or we don't; either we are willing to stand up and fight, or we are not; either we are prepared to sacrifice all for the greatest cause of all time, or we will cling to things that do not matter. Either we are focused on ourselves, or we are focused on others. Make a choice.

Time is short, and we are in that Valley of Decision that the Book of Joel speaks about just before the coming of the Lord (Joel 3:14). Count the cost – by all means, count the cost – but make the decision that counts ... no matter what the cost.

A Fool Rageth

A wise man feareth, and departeth from evil: but the fool rageth and is confident. (Proverbs 14:16)

The word "rageth" in Hebrew means a crossing over into another area. There are many connotations, but basically, this proverb is saying that fools rush in where angels fear to go. Sometimes our zeal for God exceeds our wisdom, and we trade caution for righteous passion to barge into areas we know nothing about, thinking that our intense righteousness will sustain us. But as time goes by, sometimes I feel like the more I learn, the more I realize how little I really understand.

I received an email from someone who had been given a copy of the book I wrote, and he discovered that I did not believe in a Rapture before the Tribulation. Interspersed with his resounding praises for everything I had written was a determination to set me straight on this one issue.

He had all the markings of a young Christian who had been saved long enough to feel confident in his knowledge of the Bible but not long enough to realize how much he didn't know. (Sigh) Is it like that with everyone?

I remember an old preacher telling me that when I reached 10 years old in the Lord, I would think I had arrived. Sure enough, when I had been saved for 10 years, even remembering what the preacher had said, I still felt like I had become (ahhem) an "older" Christian. How predictable is human nature!

At 20 years in the Lord, you begin to feel like you are now a big shot about to launch into the depth of your ministry, but at 30 years, you begin to wonder what happened. By the time you reach 40 years in the Lord, you are so broken that you no longer care. Only then can the Lord begin to use you in real power. Until you have surrendered all to Him, He cannot use you in the power that He has called you into because your flesh will rise to take the glory.

Of course, God uses you throughout your entire Christian life, but there is a place of broken, yielded surrender that takes years to attain. It is in that place of brokenness that Moses met his burning bush. Strong steel requires a tempering process that takes time.

As I started to answer this young man to tell him that his zeal exceeded his wisdom, I pulled back and decided to let time deal with him. His arguments were so elementary that it was obvious that he hadn't researched the issue deeply, but as I had already explained to him, I do not debate theology. Period. For all sorts of reasons.

Nevertheless, I told him about how the Lord had spoken to me when I was going to write a booklet outlining all the points from both sides of the issue to illuminate which one was correct. As I was about to sit down, the Lord spoke to me and said, "They're both wrong." They're BOTH wrong? How could they both be wrong? I quickly realized that either there was another solution that no one had thought of yet, or both sides had missed the real point and were allowing themselves to be sidetracked down paths that did not lead to the Cross but instead, to the Tree of Knowledge of Good and Evil.

That wasn't good enough for him, and he proceeded to explain to me what the Lord meant when He spoke to me.

Ah, how easily we barge through the brambles and bushes on the sides of the road in our pursuit to establish our own folly and correct all those who we have deemed wrong.

Lamentations – Something Lost

"How doth the city sit solitary, that was full of people! how is she become as a widow! she that was great among the nations, and princess among the provinces, how is she become tributary!" (Lamentations 1:1)

On Sunday, I listened to a pastor speak about how much things had changed in the last 50 years. He remembered that we once had a powerful Church that was flowing under the anointing of God where our relationships with God had been saturated in the Holy Spirit, but now we were missing the intensity of those times. Another church member commented that he couldn't remember when the last time was that he had been in a service where the intensity of the outpouring of the Holy Ghost was so strong that people were slain in the Spirit.

So, what happened?

Jeremiah faced this same challenge in Jerusalem thousands of years ago. It is part of a recurring cycle that has repeated itself since the days of Joshua – revival and apostasy, intensity and relaxation, life and death. Jeremiah saw it all -- from the revival of Josiah to the backsliding of Zedekiah, to the Lamentations for a destroyed Church.

No matter how much Jeremiah cried, pleaded, and threatened, the church of his day turned a deaf ear to the hard message of repentance, and instead turned to the prophets of peace that surrounded them. Why choose a path that will bring you to your knees and wring your soul out in weeping when you can have all the blessings of God bestowed upon you from on High for free?

Seems like a pretty simple choice to most folks. Naturally, the people of Israel chose to follow their hearts and listen to their prophets that told them the "vain and foolish things" that they wanted to hear (Lam. 2:14), not what they knew in their hearts was true. They chose their own delusions and reaped the rewards of their lusts.

The hard messages of repentance, fear of God, judgment, and hellfire, and the necessity of severe righteousness may be tolerated, but it's the rousing songs of free blessings, spiritual accommodation, and a cheap revival that gets us up on our feet cheering, singing and dancing. As Jeremiah complained, "my people love to have it so" (Jer. 5:31).

How very much like today.

The message of repentance that would bring life is nullified by the message of abundant and endless blessings -- the very vanities that ultimately cause our banishment. Nobody ever said that Satan was stupid. He's been using this same trick since the Garden of Eden, and it is still working today.

So yes, pastor, we have lost something in these last 50 years or so. It's called the Fear of God. But we chose that path ourselves when we chose a more modern, sophisticated Gospel.

We are in the belly of a cycle of apostasy that has been going on for centuries, and if we do not somehow wake up and come to a place of repentance, we will be left sitting on the ruins of the church, just like Jeremiah was.

But then, that's not what we want to hear right now, is it?

Going Home

I am sitting on a balcony outside my room overlooking the lagoon in Lagos, Nigeria. Ships slowly pass by every so often, punctuated with a smattering of river traffic and fishing boats. The sun is slowly setting, and it gives a kind of glow to the whole setting. I am finally done with my mission here. Tomorrow, I will board a plane to go home and leave the battle here for others to fight.

While I was in the grind for almost two months, there was not a day that I didn't yearn to get back home, but now that the pressure has been lifted, I can sink into a restful peace knowing that I am finished with what the Lord had called me to accomplish.

It took all of 7 weeks for me to understand the fullness of the vision that God had given me back in Texas. It seems like a lifetime ago, but it was only a few months since the Lord gave me a vision of the country of Nigeria lying under a cloud of thick darkness with little pinpricks of light crying out for help.

When I first arrived, the mission seemed simple, almost routine, but as I waded through battle after battle and victory after victory, I began to see deeper and farther than when I had first received the vision. This was not just a battle for Nigeria's soul, but for all of Africa, and ultimately the world.

I have always believed that there will be one last great revival just before the Coming of the Lord. According to the Book of Joel, the Christians that God will raise up will be the strongest Christians since the beginning of time (Joel 2:2), and He will send the greatest outpouring ever seen (Joel 2:23). I believe that last great revival will start here in Africa and will generate from Nigeria and Kenya.

But Satan will not roll over and allow Joel's Army to rise up without a fight, and that fight will be as intense as the outpouring of God. This is war, and the cutting edge of the front line is here in Nigeria.

God will raise up shepherds after His own heart, and He will raise up leaders and generals who will get their authority from the deep, embracing Fear of God, and will stand head and shoulders over the self-proclaimed titled church nobility that is in charge today. And while the move of God will be set on fire among the small churches that genuinely seek the face of God, it will be the large, prosperous cathedrals that, like Joseph's 10 brethren, will persecute them. That's the way it always happens.

As for myself, I have struck the matches and lit the fires that I was called to light. I have dropped them in a savanna of dry grass, and there they will burn. I honestly believe what God told me before I ever left Texas to come here – He told me that they will not remember me. I would simply be the Johnny Appleseed who ran through the countryside planting seed and lighting fires.

But one of these days, in one of these little churches, someone will say something -- maybe a broken-hearted testimony, maybe a piercing message, maybe a prayer of repentance for the church – somewhere, someone, somehow there will be a breaking of hearts, and the sound of the snap will be heard in Heaven and the fire of God will fall, and Africa will be set ablaze. And it will burn so hot that we will feel the heat around the world.

And an old man will sit on his porch in a little town in Texas and will smile.

The Christmas Nail

> *"But he was wounded for our transgressions,*
> *he was bruised for our iniquities:*
> *the chastisement of our peace was upon him;*
> *and with his stripes we are healed.*
>
> *All we like sheep have gone astray;*
> *we have turned every one to his own way;*
> *and the Lord hath laid on him the iniquity of us all."*
>
> *(Isaiah 53:5-6)*

I have an old iron spike that is my most precious Christmas tree ornament. Nothing fancy. Just an old metal spike with a bright red satin ribbon tied to it so I can hang it on my tree. It's not polished, and it doesn't shine; just an old pitted, dull gun-metal grey spike about 10" long, but it is hung with the utmost care.

Every year I hang this Christmas Nail on a sturdy branch near the trunk, a branch that will hold such a spike without being noticed by well-wishers who drop by to admire our gaily decorated tree. There is none of the glitz of the other ornaments, tinsel, or swirl of lights, none of the prominence of the angel that sits atop the tree, and none of the excitement of the wrapped presents below.

The nail is known only to me and my family and understood only by the heart that knows it true significance.

I never want to forget what Jesus did for us. I never want to be so caught up in the spirit of Christmas celebration and gaiety that I become overwhelmed with the good cheer, the presents, and even that spirit of love for one another that we all feel in the air during this time and forget the price that was paid for Christmas.

Over the years, I have written my traditional column about why I believe in Christmas -- not the specifics of the date as much as the witness of God's presence during this holiday season. No other time during the year can we taste a feeling of the unfathomable love of God for mankind like we do at Christmastime. There's something special about this time that cannot be explained any other way than by the presence of the Holy Spirit to give mankind hope that God gave His only Son so we could have life. It's as if God gives us a taste of Heaven.

But I never want to forget the price that was paid for Christmas.

The Christmas tree is but a picture of the Christ-tree which only He could decorate for us, ornamented with nails like this.

The Esther Church

> *"And the king loved Esther above all the women, and she obtained grace and favor in his sight more than all the virgins; so that he set the royal crown upon her head, and made her queen instead of Vashti." (Esther 2:17)*

I like to read Bible in the morning because it always seems so much fresher when I first wake up. This morning I was drawn to the Book of Esther, which has always held a special place in my heart.

Esther is a picture of the true Church, the Bride that the Lord has chosen above all others. The king chose her above all others, not because of all the ornaments and worldly enhancements that we so readily adorn ourselves with, but because of her natural beauty and the purity of her heart. She was so different from all the others that King Ahasuerus didn't bother to see anyone else after he gazed upon her.

Oh, how the king loved her! I can see reminisces of the Song of Solomon in his love for her, and her for him. Esther entered that special place in the king's heart that is only reserved for those who have become one with him.

She resided in a wonderful place of beauty in the king's palace and had need of nothing. Her one desire was to be with her king in that blessed place as his queen and would have continued there in peace and blessings forever. There were other currents at work in realms of darkness, however, that were set to destroy her tranquility.

While Esther sat in the palace, Mordecai sat in sackcloth and ashes in the king's gate. Wicked Haman had plotted to destroy the people of God and was willing to marshal everything he had to accomplish his demonic intentions.

Although Esther loved her people, she was insulated from the realities of the spiritual war that was poised to destroy them. Mordecai knew; Esther did not.

These are the two churches: one that is enveloped in the blessings of God, and one that faces the sufferings of the Body of Christ. While many of us want all the good things of God and have a genuine love for the entire Body of believers, we are often unaware of what our brothers and sisters in the persecuted church must endure. It's not that we don't care; it's that we don't know.

And yet, if Satan's plans for destruction were to succeed, it would not only destroy the persecuted church, but would reach even into the palace where the church of Esther resides. Our own salvation is dependent upon a victory over the battle opposing our brethren who must face the onslaught of wickedness.

Mordecai knew this. It is why he sat in the king's gate crying out to God for deliverance. His words to Esther were chilling:

> *Think not with thyself that thou shalt escape in the king's house, more than all the Jews. For if thou altogether holdest thy peace at this time, then shall there enlargement and deliverance arise to the Jews from another place; but thou and thy father's house shall be destroyed: and who knoweth whether thou art come to the kingdom for such a time as this?*
>
> *(Esther 4:13-14)*

America is blessed as no other nation on Earth. Our blessings come not just from hard work and creativity, but from the blessings that God has put upon us as a country that was originally established upon the Gospel of Jesus Christ to be a lighthouse to the world.

But what have we exported to our brethren outside the palace?

They need more than messages of "be thou warmed and filled" from us. The one complaint that I heard over and over in Africa was that the messages from America all have to do with money and prosperity, but what they need are messages that will strengthen the soul of their church.

Living inside the palace walls may be wonderful, but what our Mordecai brethren hunger for is deliverance from a war that we neither know about nor understand. Money won't deliver them from Haman – only the power of God will. And we, as an Esther-type of church must place our hearts, not our money, on the line to go before the Throne of God for them and touch the golden scepter.

Mary at Christmas

> *And behold, there was a man in Jerusalem, whose name was Simeon; and the same man was just and devout, waiting for the consolation of Israel: and the Holy Ghost was upon him. And it was revealed unto him by the Holy Ghost, that he should not see death before he had seen the Lord's Christ.*
>
> *(Luke 2:25,26)*

Thirty-three years later, the old man Simeon was gone, and Mary was the sole survivor of all the witnesses of the birth of God's Messiah. This great event of the birth of Christ was the advent of a plan that had its beginning before Creation, and that had been spoken of by the prophets and dreamed of by all Israel for thousands of years.

The Savior of the world had finally arrived, but who was there to witness this greatest of all events? Three wise men, a handful of shepherds (and maybe a drummer boy), an old woman prophetess, and Simeon. Besides Joseph and Mary, very few people knew what had just happened, and fewer still understood the magnitude of it.

As Simeon returned the baby to Mary, he must have looked deeply into her eyes as he realized that she alone of all these witnesses would remain at the end. He and the prophetess Anna were old, the shepherds were scattered, and the wise men had returned to their homes. Even Joseph would be gone. Only Mary would be left.

Thirty-three years later, as she knelt at the foot of a cross on Golgotha and gazed up at her son, did her heart go back to those few precious moments so many years before when she held the promise of all mankind in her arms, and a cloud of witnesses surrounded her to testify that this indeed was the Son of God? Now they were all gone, and she alone was left as the sole witness that His was truly a virgin birth, that this really was God in Man who had come to save the world.

But now, he hung upon a rough wooden cross, rejected by the church, the government, and the people. Only a handful of outcasts clung to Him in the last dying moments, while all the crowds who had witnessed His mighty works had fled. How many had once believed but now had become troubled with doubt and had turned away, leaving her to weep for Him on top of that lonely hill? Even His disciples had fled.

Did she ever complain? Did she ever once deny that His birth was truly the supernatural work of the Holy Spirit? Never. Her silence was her strongest witness, for she of all people knew who He really was and that the mission He came to accomplish could only end this way. He had come to die.

As we gather round the Christmas tree and recite to our children the meaning of Christmas, let us never forget the young Jewish girl who once held God's gift to mankind in her arms and, through her suffering at the foot of the Cross, gave the world an enduring witness that truly He was the Son of God.

Thank God for His wonderful gift and the price that was paid to give it to us.

Abraham and Abimelech

> *"And Abraham said of Sarah his wife, she is my sister: and Abimelech king of Gerar sent, and took Sarah. But God came to Abimelech in a dream by night, and said to him, Behold, thou art but a dead man, for the woman which thou has taken; for she is a man's wife."*
> (Genesis 20:2-3)

I'll bet there was some scurrying around in Abimelech's house the next morning!

All Abimelech was looking for was an heir for his throne, and Sarah looked like a good candidate for the job. He could sense the blessing that had been placed upon her by the Lord when Abraham had been visited by God and his two angels just before going on to destroy Sodom. When an anointing is placed upon you, those who are around you can sense it – they may not understand it, but they can feel it -- and Sarah had that anointing. And it also didn't hurt that not only was she pretty, but she appeared to be available.

Abraham was a great man of faith, even the Father of Faith, but this was an incident of weakness for him. Here was a man who had defeated kings, had been visited supernaturally by God himself more than once, had received great promises from Him, and had the manifest mantle of blessings placed over him – but he was afraid of Abimelech?

Satan doesn't play fair. In his demonic intelligence, Satan knew that Sarah would begin the lineage that would lead to the Messiah. The promise had been given, and a child would soon be on the way. What better way to break the plan of Salvation than to defile the mother of the seed and take her away from

Abraham? Who knows the enormous pressure of fears and panic that Satan applied to Abraham during this time?

The same thing happened to Jacob, who, after being visited by God to go to Bethel, lost his confidence in God's protection and feared his brother Esau's arrival. It is something we all go through at one time or another.

Before any great move of God, there will be an enormous onslaught from the devil that is designed to derail God's plan. Since God uses people as His anointed vessels to bring about His plan, the devil will focus his attack on those same men and women. His primary weapon is to try to undermine and destroy their faith in God's Providence.

It is easy to say that Abraham should have trusted God. After all, look at how many personal, supernatural experiences he had experienced with God Almighty. But spiritual warfare does not operate on common sense. It operates on the spiritual strength that you have now. Satan will wait until he sees a time of weakness on your part before he tries to cover you with his blanket of fears, doubts, and darkness to destroy your faith in God.

Abraham was probably buried with unnamed fears and panic that seemed to come out of nowhere. The solid ground that his faith walked upon had become slippery quicksand, the closeness he had felt with God had vanished, and his clarity of sight had become clouded over, just as David said in Psalms, "like a bottle in the smoke."

It is in times like these that we are tested, tried, and taught. We are forced to examine our walk with God and the strength of our beliefs. When we finally get through the darkness of each valley, we find our faith has been made stronger than before.

Abraham needed to go through this valley before the Lord would bring him his heir, Isaac. He had to see the powerful deliverance of God so that faith in God's promise to him would to be girded with strength and would establish with bedrock faith that through this son would come God's greatest promise to mankind – Salvation.

Abraham never doubted again.

When you begin to descend into your next valley, remember that the shadow that is cast over you is merely a shadow – the sun is still shining on the other side, and that every descent also has its final ascent and that you will come out at the other end.

But most of all, remember that it is through those times of struggle like these that God establishes His promises.

Nathan

> *"And these were born unto him in Jerusalem; Shimea, and Shobab, and Nathan, and Solomon, four, of Bathshua the daughter of Ammiel"*
>
> *(1st Chronicles 3:5)*

One of the interesting things about being alive is that there is a lot of stuff you still don't know.

I know that Jesus Christ could not come through the seed of Jeconiah because of the curse set upon him in Jeremiah 22 that no one of his seed would sit upon the Throne of David. And yet, Joseph, Mary's husband, was of Jeconiah's lineage. The answer? A virgin birth, of course!

So, whose lineage did Mary come through so that Jesus would still be of the seed of David? Out of all his sons, it came through Nathan, the brother of Solomon.

Now, this strikes me as a little odd. Who was Nathan? The only times he is ever mentioned is when he is listed as one of the sons of Bathsheba and in an obscure verse in Zechariah 12:12. That's not exactly an impressive resume considering all the other big shots amongst David's other sons. It's as if the Lord just swept all of them off the table and only focused on the two youngest sons in David's entire flock.

Isn't it funny how we focus on the things that seem so impressive while God picks lowly things to do His great works? God just doesn't do things the way we would. We try to figure everything out so we can accomplish great things, but God works by faith.

I don't know about you, but that is encouraging to me. I can look around me and see all the wonderful things that so many great men in God have accomplished and still know that, in the final analysis, it is not the great works that <u>we</u> do that impresses God, but the great faith that we have in the works that <u>He</u> does that matters.

I have no idea why God picked Nathan for the lineage of Jesus Christ, but I'm sure there's an answer that will be revealed someday. Until then, it is reassuring to know that you don't have to be a big shot to be part of His Plan, even if the rest of the world is not impressed. You just have to have faith that God knows exactly what He is doing in your life, even if you don't.

You just have to trust God.

Passing on the Glory

"We will not hide them from their children, shewing to the generation to come the praises of the Lord, and his strength, and his wonderful works that he hath done...That they might set their hope in God, and not forget the works of God, but keep his commandments."

(Psalms 78)

Oh, the Glory! Can any of you out there remember what it was like to feel the outpouring of the Holy Ghost filling up services with His Shekinah Glory? Do you remember when God came down, and hearts were overwhelmed, and praises poured out from open hearts? Remember when souls were filled to overflowing, and the Spirit of God flowed like an anointing oil through our streets? Souls were saved, people were healed, and multitudes were drawn to the fountain of life pouring out from the Throne.

Those who are out there that remember know what I'm talking about.

Where has it gone? What happened to the great moves of God in our churches? Those who should have passed on the glory have instead given us over to man-made doctrines, to secular preaching, and to churches that have lost their vibrancy. The experience of walking in the depths of the Spirit of God has been lost. In its place, we now have educated preachers who know so much theology about God that they no longer know what it's like to be led by the Spirit. If that is not so, then where is the manifestation of the Power of God? And why is there such a reliance on books and theological studies?

The Kingdom of God is not in word but in power, but we have turned the Gospel of Jesus Christ into just another religion. Lost souls that are desperate for God look upon what we preach as just another philosophy about God. Just another dead religion with no power, no Spirit, and no glory.

Their cry is *"Sir, we would see Jesus!"* (John 12:21). Give us the demonstration of the Spirit and power (1 Cor. 2:4). Let Holy Ghost conviction open our hearts to return to that place in God that we once had. Church "as usual" is death. We need Life! And that can only come from men of God who are not afraid to take a stand for righteousness and who are willing to walk the walk of the lowly Nazarene and allow their lives to be filled with the power of God instead of theology.

The indictment stands against those who remember and who did not pass it on.

Puritans

> *"And, behold, there met him a woman with the attire of an harlot, and subtil of heart ... So she caught him, and kissed him, and with an impudent face said unto him, I have peace offerings with me; this day have I paid my vows. Therefore came I forth to meet thee, diligently to seek thy face, and I have found thee."*
>
> *(Proverbs 7:10-15)*

I have been reading about the early New England forefathers, who, in the face of incredible adversities, had, for the first time in history, established a colony based on the Word of God. The hardships, death, and hunger which turned many others away only served to compact them in their resolve to overcome and establish the Light of Jesus Christ in a dark continent that would, in turn, shine as a testimony to the rest of the world.

But what happened to the Puritans? Where have they gone?

Within a generation or so, the foundations of their covenant began to crumble. Their children, who had not gone through the harsh, refining fire that their parents had gone through, began to weaken in their resolve to remain holy and true to the God who had established and prospered them in this New World.

Prosperity has a way of doing that to even the most resolute of souls.

As Puritan Elder Cotton Mather bitingly put it, "Religion begat prosperity, and the daughter devoured the mother."

Faith, tested by the fire of adversity, will foster the blessings of God, and those blessings will minister an entrance into prosperity. But the procession rarely ends there.

Prosperity often becomes an ugly stepdaughter who, with a painted face, becomes a seductive harlot. She stands on the street corner, wooing us with assurances that she has paid her vows, and invites us to her perfumed bed of ivory to solace ourselves with love. The simple hear and follow like an ox going to the slaughter.

When I pray for the American Church, I do not pray for God to bless her. I pray for adversity.

Our society is full of good men and women who desire to do good things, but God is not looking for good men and women. He is looking for bad men and women who depend upon Him for His goodness, not their own, for it is the goodness of God, not the blessings, that leads us to repentance.

The Substance of Faith

> *These all died in faith, not having received the promises, but having seen them afar off, and were persuaded of them, and embraced them, and confessed that they were strangers and pilgrims on the earth. For they that say such things declare plainly that they seek a country.*
> *(Hebrews 11:13,14)*

Faith has always been something that I have wondered about. I'm talking about real Faith, not just belief. There is a difference between faith and belief, but the very essence of true faith is hard to crystallize into concrete terms.

The Israelites in the Wilderness believed God – boy, did they believe! – but that wasn't enough. These people had walked through two walls of water to escape slavery, had seen the miracles done in the desert, and if that wasn't enough, had even heard God Himself speak from the mountain out of the thundering and lightning. They ate food that fell out of heaven every day, and all they had to do was look outside the tent flap to see a pillar of cloud by day and a pillar of fire by night. Don't tell me they didn't believe.

And yet, they entered not into the Promise Land because of unbelief.

There's a difference between faith and belief that escapes the cursory glance. Faith is much deeper than pointing to the sky and saying, "Yep, there's a God up there!"

I'm not a good example of blind faith. It took some incredible supernatural experiences for me to believe in God at all, much less Jesus Christ, and then throughout my Christian walk, the Lord has had to keep bolstering me with more supernatural experiences to anchor my faith. I believe in God because of the stark physical evidence that I have seen and experienced, not because I wanted to believe or because that's how I was raised.

I thought I would pass that reliance on empirical evidence on to my students when I taught high school, but I still remember the answer a girl in my class gave me when I had challenged the class to answer why they believed in God. Her answer to my challenge? She looked me dead in my eyes and said, "I just have Faith."

'Nuff said. I sheepishly picked up my jaw that had dropped to the ground. What do you say to that? It wasn't blind belief that had answered me; it was something deeper that exuded out of the very depths of her soul. She had faith in God – something I had trouble grasping.

Faith is something more than believing. It goes into realms of the heart and soul that pierce into heavenly places where the carnal mind cannot follow. It plugs into something beyond this world and transforms a person from the inside out. It is the substance of things hoped for.

When you have crossed over into true Faith, your entire outlook changes. No longer does the world hold anything of lasting fascination for you. Your home, your real home, gets a dramatic change of address. Faith plants an anchor for your soul in celestial ground that, although you can't explain it, analyze it, or understand it, becomes the new destination of your life. You no longer reside in this world – you have become a Pilgrim, and you are just passing through.

I sat back the other day trying to figure out why I have this desire to serve the Lord. It's not the rewards of Heaven that get me going because I really don't know what is up there. God has not given us that many scriptures to rely upon for any vivid description of Heaven. I have heard several people describe the visions they have had, and that gives you an idea, but it isn't like God is running a marketing campaign for vacation homes after you die. I'm not doing this because of what I am going to get after I die.

Now, the prospect of spending eternity in a burning Hell, on the other hand, does grab my attention. The specter of Hell has won many souls because it rips open that nebulous curtain that the world drapes over us to expose the stark reality of what is on the other side, but to be honest, that is not what drives me either. I'm not going to Hell – I don't care what I have to do to escape it – I am not going there, so that is not the thing that drives me and pushes me on, either.

I'm not sure what it is. I guess, like that girl in my class, I have chosen to have Faith, and it is Faith that has made the difference. The supernatural experiences, the incredible proofs in the Word of God, the obvious ways God moves in our lives, and even the confirmations of common sense are only external manifestations of a faith that has latched on to something far beyond this world.

Faith is the substance of things hoped for, the evidence of things not seen that transforms you as you reach through the shroud of this world to touch the Throne of God.

Timex

Give a portion to seven, and also to eight; for thou knowest not what evil shall be upon the earth.

(Ecclesiastes 11:2)

Tick, tick, tick, tick....

Unlike Timex watches, there is a point when time will stop ticking. Our nature is such that we relegate that point in time to somewhere way off in the distant future. Yeah, it will happen, but not tomorrow. It's way out there somewhere, but the immediacy of that moment is not striking enough to cause a high level of concern. And so, we go about our normal routine, taking care of the things in our daily lives that do have a sense of immediacy.

Is there a time when we will get ready for a coming time of desolation?

Perhaps we are waiting for a warning bell from the Lord. But aren't there enough warning bells written in the Word of God for all of us to read and consider? The chilling answer is that He tells us that He will come as a thief in the night.

While you scurry about getting your own life together, don't lose track of time. Certainly, it's important to pay our bills, prepare our careers, make provisions for our children's education, and all the other things that we consider important. Just remember the things that are important, and don't leave them after you've taken care of everything else. You may find out too late that the time will be over and your resources spent.

I believe we have a small window of opportunity to accomplish whatever we are going to do for the Lord. Events may snowball into an avalanche of prophecy fulfillments which will spin your normal life out of control. There is a point coming when you will no longer be allowed to stand up and proclaim the Gospel. What will you do then?

Your financial problems may have been solved, but will that matter if it was at the cost of lost souls? What happens when your personal life has been organized, but now you can no longer stand up for the Gospel of Jesus Christ because the persecution is so intense? How will you stand if you have spent your time getting the details of your life together but neglected the spiritual preparation that will give you the strength to go to the Cross?

Think that's an unfair, harsh scenario? Think again. That's exactly what is coming – sooner rather than later. Better we should give that portion now while we can, because you have no idea what is coming, neither do you have any idea how soon.

Once it's too late, it's too late.

Go to the ant, thou sluggard; consider her ways, and be wise: (Proverbs 6:6)

Where's the Line?

I wonder about a lot of things.

It's not that I am the naturally curious type that wonders about everything that comes along, like some overly playful cat, but some things warrant answers that are more important than the humdrum procession of daily living. One of those things is where God will draw the line between those who go to Heaven and those who will wind up in Hell.

I figure that's a pretty important question – more important than even where my next meal is coming from, how I will pay the bills, or who is going to win the Super Bowl. Since I will have to live with that answer for Eternity, I want to make sure I get it right.

When I look at standard Christianity, I see a few basic levels:

One is the average good-guy Christian who lives a decent life, works hard for an honest living, treats others with a certain measure of respect and kindness, and will admit to believing in God ... if you ask him. He's a regular nice guy, and yeah, maybe he says "hell" or "damn" once in a while, but other than that, he keeps most of the rules in the Bible that he has been taught. You can meet this guy every Sunday in church, holding his Bible and singing worship songs. He's been saved once upon a time and considers himself a good Christian that is on his way to Heaven. But that is about it.

Of course, that's a lot better than the mass of people out there who, despite the fact that they curse, lie, drink, fornicate, dabble in pornography, and tell dirty jokes, still think that they're going to Heaven simply because they believe in God – as if that is the only requirement for escaping Hell. Most of them have never studied the Word of God to find out how strict the rules really are but are content to have other like-minded believers convince them that they are going to Heaven, nonetheless.

Shucks, <u>everybody</u> thinks they're going to Heaven, even the most destitute. If you think I'm kidding, just ask them. They'll tell you that Jesus loves them and that they really aren't such a bad person once you get to know them. If that's the case, then why did Jesus have to die?

Then there's a small group of people who are driven by more than a desire to go to church and sing songs. They have a driving passion that engulfs their entire life to separate themselves from the "stuff" of this world because all they want is God. These are the fanatics that we tolerate but politely dismiss as being just a bit over the edge. It's not enough for them to just live a quiet Christian life – they have to convince everybody else to get as intense as they are.

They can be irritating, especially when you have settled into a normal life and quietly believe in God for your salvation. It's as if they are on a different wavelength and insist that everyone needs to turn on the same light switch. They're just a different kind of people that act like they can see something that most of us normal people just don't see. Why they can't just let the rest of us go on in our own ways is beyond what most of us can understand.

But then, maybe they do see something that is covered by the daily routine of this life. Maybe that fire that seems to burn inside them wasn't kindled from an over-active imagination but is something that they caught from the Throne of God.

So back to the original question – where exactly does God draw the line? How high does God set the bar? Hell burns for a long time, so you better make sure you have the right answer.

Is it simply a matter of what we think – a function of our own determination – or is Life a test to see if we will look beyond what is convenient to seek the face of God for the Truth?

It's a good question.

Someone once asked Jesus the same question --

Then said one unto him, Lord, are there few that be saved? And he said unto them, Strive to enter in at the strait gate: for many, I say unto you, will seek to enter in, and shall not be able.

(Luke 13:23,24)

Amazed

> *And he will destroy in this mountain the face of the covering cast over all people, and the vail that is spread over all nations.*
>
> *He will swallow up death in victory; and the Lord GOD will wipe away tears from off all faces; and the rebuke of his people shall he take away from off all the earth: for the LORD hath spoken it.*
>
> *And it shall be said in that day, Lo, this is our God; we have waited for him, and he will save us:*
>
> (Isaiah 25:7-9)

After so many years, I am still amazed at the fact that there really is a God. A lot of people seem to have been born with a bedrock faith in God, and their acceptance of the existence of God seems to be as natural as breathing. They can easily reach out and touch the substance of faith.

But I was never that way.

The whole concept of God has always been difficult for me to grasp. I guess it's just that the physical reality of this world we live in is so different than the spiritual reality of Heaven that I have always had trouble syncing them up. I can't wait to have that covering ripped off that is cast over all people so I can step into that eternal reality. But for now, it sometimes seems so otherworldly.

Now, you might be surprised to hear that from someone who has given over 50 years of his life to serving the Lord, but the truth is that I know God exists, not because I have blind faith or because I figured it out, or because it makes sense, but because of the supernatural experiences that I have had over those 50 years – and there has been plenty of them.

I was an atheistic college kid when God first revealed Himself to me in a supernatural revelation. What a shock to find out He was there! But even with such a supernatural event, within a week, I was beginning to think I was just going nuts. So, God had to shock me again. And again. I was a pretty hard nut to crack, and I often wonder why He had such patience with me.

So, my faith is based on reality. Yeah, I know that's not the Biblical definition of faith, but that's just the way it is for me. I've felt the Holy Spirit in powerful outpourings in prayer, and I've seen the power of God fall in those old powerhouse Holy Ghost services that we used to have years ago. I have had supernatural revelations in His Word, I've had real visions, and I have actually heard God speak to me (just like us speaking to each other but without sound). I've laid hands on the sick and seen hundreds of miracle healings. It doesn't matter if no one else believes He is there. I <u>know</u> He is there. I don't have to figure it out – I have touched the Throne of God.

It's like opening the door to a room and seeing God standing there. It doesn't matter what things look like outside that room when you close the door. I know He is inside that room. You can tell me all you want that it doesn't make sense or that science has successfully proven that God is not there, but I've been able to look inside that room too many times, and guess what? He's still there.

But I am still amazed. There's a place called Heaven, and it really exists. There's also a place called Hell, and there are people there right now screaming in agony. It doesn't matter that I can't see any of it – it's there because He is.

And then I turn on the TV and heard supposedly intelligent men scoff at the idea of an All-powerful Creator who just--

poof! -- created the world. They expostulate for hours with intelligent-sounding scientific facts to try and make us look stupid, but the fact remains that God is still there.

No matter how hard you try to reason around it, He is still there. And He is not going away no matter how stupid someone thinks the whole idea of a real living God sounds.

I know because that was me 52 years ago. And I am still amazed.

Her candle goeth not out by night.

I am struck by this passage about the virtuous woman in Proverbs 31:18. Who burns their candle all night long? And why would you do that? I dare say that most of us turn the lights off when we go to bed. But not the virtuous woman. She keeps her light burning throughout the entire night.

As Christians, we rejoice in our salvation and celebrate our transformation from Death, but a truly converted Christian will not stop there. He will look back into the darkness and shine a light so others can see the lighthouse of safety and come out of that world of death.

Those who have been truly transformed by grace are not satisfied with attending bland church services, fellowshipping with other satisfied believers in ivory halls of contentment, and warming themselves by the coals of indifference. Something inside them cannot rest while others are dying. The realities of darkness become stark when seen from the place of light. The dark seems darker, and the despair seems more desperate. While some seek the calm serenity of their chapels and cathedrals, others want to set up a rescue station one foot away from the very Gates of Hell. Light the candle and let it burn all night long!

Our efforts to shine a light aren't in answer to a religious directive or obedience to a doctrinal precept. It is not works for works sake. It is the very heart of grace.

We assume that works are the antithesis of grace, but that is not so. Works are the evidence of grace. Just as charity is much more than "love," grace is much more than the superficial quip of "undeserved mercy." Grace is the fountain from which mercy flows. It is what gives birth to charity, and charity is the very essence of the entire Gospel, the main theme of the Cross, the whole reason why Jesus died, and the central reason why we were called to salvation. Without Charity, we are but tinkling bells and a sounding cymbal – plenty of noise and pretty music, but lacking substance.

Grace is not only the flame of the virtuous woman's candle and the source of light, but it is that which gave her the desire to light it and let it burn all night long.

Solomon's Love Affair

> *The song of songs, which is Solomon's.*
>
> *Let him kiss me with the kisses of his mouth: for thy love is better than wine.*
>
> *Because of the savour of thy good ointments thy name is as ointment poured forth, therefore do the virgins love thee.*
>
> *Draw me, we will run after thee: the king hath brought me into his chambers: we will be glad and rejoice in thee, we will remember thy love more than wine: the upright love thee.*
>
> *(Song of Solomon 1:1-4)*

Someone recently asked me when I had first decided to enter the ministry. I don't know that there is a specific instant in time that I can point to when I made any decision. It just always was.

The closest thing I can relate it to is when I first saw Cindy.

We were having services every evening and twice on Sundays, so literally hundreds of people were passing through that little church, and I paid little attention to any of them other than that they were souls that needed salvation. No one stood out to me on a personal basis. And then I saw her standing in the back of the congregation.

Although I tried desperately to dismiss it, not pay attention to it, and somehow get around it, the course of my life was set. I was hooked. And after 45 years of marriage, I am still hooked.

My relationship with God has been the same. From the point of salvation, the direction of my life was inalterably set. I was in love. I had become married to Jesus Christ, and my whole world had changed.

Solomon understood what that was like. He wrote about the greatest love affair the world has ever known – the love that God has for His Bride and her love for Him. It is all-consuming - something through which all the rest of your existence is measured. You now look at life through a lens that colors every other thing in relation to your love toward God.

Does anything else matter in your life? Do you care if you become king of the world or a janitor sweeping the church floor? All other things – fame, fortune, and honor – kneel in subjection to your marriage to Him. God becomes the love of your life.

So often, we see others who do not have that same depth of intensity in their Christianity. They lay claim to salvation and go through all the motions of a wife keeping house for her husband, but the passion of love has waned. It becomes duty rather than desire. How sad to see something so beautiful become so dull.

Church, without passion, can become a bland, tasteless porridge that is eaten without zeal. We eat because we should, and the taste is, uh, okay, but the fireworks of a fiesta are gone. It's just, as I call it, "church as usual."

I want to be part of a church that has such a passion that a simple meal is turned into a feast that is so exciting that you want to invite everyone you meet to this great celebration and meet this wonderful husband with whom you are so much in love with that you can't contain your excitement.

There is more to church than showing up at a meeting house, just as there is more to a marriage than cleaning the house and making the bed. Salvation was meant to be the all-consuming passion of your life, so much so that it can only be related to falling headlong in love with the person of your dreams. Anything short of that is missing the most wonderful thing in life.

Behold, thou art fair, my love; behold, thou art fair;
(Song of Solomon 1:15)

Lazarus

> *Jesus therefore again groaning in himself cometh to the grave. It was a cave, and a stone lay upon it. Jesus said, Take ye away the stone. (John 11:38,39)*

The raising of Lazarus from the dead was one of the most notable miracles that Jesus did, but the greater importance of this miracle was not about Lazarus but that it set in motion the events that would lead to Jesus' crucifixion.

As Christians, we tend to seek after the good things that we hope God will do for us. God is good, we acknowledge, and so, therefore, God is supposed to do good things for us. But underlying the theme of victory throughout the Bible is the message that victory comes through brokenness to God.

Many think that since Jesus suffered, we don't have to. The victory was won on the Cross and was a finished work. All we have to do is follow along in His wake, and we will receive the blessings. Unfortunately, that is a result of only a cursory skimming over the Scriptures without realizing that God has called us to that same crucified walk so that He can work that same victory in us.

Brokenness is the process by which God empties the "you" out of you. He breaks the resistance of our will and our ways out of us so that we will come to a final place of surrender. Only when He has a clean, transparent, and empty vessel that is broken from our own ways will He have in His hands something that is as yielded as soft putty that He can now fashion into a vessel of His likeness. Only then can He fill us with His glory so that, like transparent glass, empty and fashioned in His likeness, people no longer see us; they see the glory of the Almighty God in us and can be drawn to Him.

There is an old saying that God requires a price from us that flesh does not want to pay. We can choose to settle into a comfortable rut to escape the price of a deep subjection that He places before us. That is our choice. But if we ever expect to rise to a place in God where He can use us in any great and mighty way, we must face the path of the Cross and all that goes along with that rough road to the Calvary in our own lives.

Abraham faced it when asked to sacrifice his only son. Jacob faced it on his long 20-year road to go back to Bethel. Joseph faced it in a forgotten cell in a dismal Egyptian prison. And Moses faced it on the backside of a desert, taking care of someone else's flock. There is a path set before each of us that none of us relish facing because all we can see at this end is the suffering that we will have to go through to get to the other end. But Jacob would never have become Israel, Joseph would never have become a ruler of Egypt, Moses would never have delivered the children of Israel, and Jesus Christ would never have broken the power of sin if they hadn't gone down that road.

Jesus knew when He raised Lazarus from the dead that it would lead to His death on the Cross, but He chose that path willingly because He could see past the suffering and saw our faces. He was made perfect through suffering.

When all Hell assails us, as the song goes, the flesh always fails us. But when we allow God to lead us through the struggles we have before us and trust that God has a plan for our lives, He will walk with us through those valleys. No matter how dark they are, no matter how hard they seem, no matter how deep they go, no matter how unfair they seem, no matter how much pain is there, we follow the footsteps of those who have gone on before us and who paved the way so that we could be brought to Salvation.

And leading the way are the footprints of the feet of Jesus, the captain of our salvation, who tasted death for every man that we might have life.

Whole Duty of Man

> *Let us hear the conclusion of the whole matter: Fear God, and keep his commandments: for this is the whole duty of man. (Ecclesiastes 12:13)*

Sounds simple, doesn't it? All the lofty intricacies of religion and philosophy, all the stress in pursuing our goals, and all the multiple complexities of life have been reduced to this one verse.

So why have we made life so complicated? Because those are the two things that we don't want to do.

We do not want to fear God; we want Him to be our Daddy. God is love, so what that means to the bulk of our modern spiritualist pastors today is that our spirituality should be beautiful and full of love and flowers. We should not have to be afraid of God.

The messages we love the most from our preachers are about blessings, peace, and joy – all the good stuff. We want to hear how God wants to bless us, not how we should stand in fear and trembling before Him. We will flock in great numbers to whoever will preach a message like that to us and send them money to support those golden calves.

But the fear of God that was prescribed in the Old Testament is the same that is prescribed in the New Testament. Moses, the only man that God talked to face-to-face, feared God so much his knees smote together (Heb. 12:21). David, the apple of God's eye, said that the flesh trembled for fear of Him (Psalms 119:120). The holy prophets spoke of God being their dread (Isa. 8:13).

Is the New Testament any different? Hardly. Paul said that knowing the terror of the Lord, we, therefore, persuade men (2

Cor. 5:11) and that we should serve the Lord with fear and trembling (Eph. 6:5), knowing that our God is a consuming fire (Heb. 12:29). Yikes!

But today, we translate the fear of God as "awesome respect." Maybe we're just made of better dirt than our ancestors were, or maybe, because this generation is so much smarter than they were, things are different for us. Who knows? Whatever the reason, we have certainly mollified that message of fear to something that is much more marketable and palatable for today's congregations and TV audiences.

As for the commandments of God, well, we have different agendas today, so things apply differently to us. Since we have to deal with today's sophisticated world instead of the old primitive tribal societies from when the Bible was written, God surely understands that we are not subject to the same constraints as they were. Divorce is not as big a deal, sex is commonly understood as acceptable (as long as it is with only your current partner, of course), deceit can be excused if it's only a white lie or is for a good cause, and cheating on taxes is expected because the IRS isn't fair. Hey, it's all relative, isn't it?

Oh, and don't worry, if we cross the line somewhere, we can rest assured that because God is Love (see the first premise above), we can always ask God, and He will forgive us every time we ask. As long as you've said the Sinners Prayer once in your life, you're eternally sealed into Heaven, so it isn't a big deal anyway.

Geez, what a good God He is! Cheap, easy, and fun – what else could you want? It's like having your very own fairy Godmother.

I have listened to people who, while wallowing in sin, still tell me that they are going to Heaven because they believe in

God. Why? Because that's what they have been told, and it's what they wanted to hear, so they believe it.

But it is not what the Bible says.

The Bible is not generational; it is universal and eternal. You will burn in the same Hell, shoulder to shoulder, with all the other guys who broke the same commandments throughout time.

The Bible clearly states that it is by the fear of the Lord that men depart from evil (Prov. 16:6). Without it, men will not be driven to the Cross for salvation. And without salvation, we have no power to overcome sin. The problem is that we hardly ever hear about the fear of God anymore, and when we do, it is always in an intellectual capacity, or as Isaiah puts it, "by the precept of men," not with their hearts (Isa. 29:13).

Yes, it can all be reduced to the simplicity of one verse. Satan knows this, so he has done everything he could to take away the one thing that God has asked us to do. He knows that when, like mesmerized children, we follow our fleshly hearts and succumb to teachers who will lead us away from the fear of God, we relinquish our power to overcome sin.

And that is why Hell hath enlarged itself.

Retail Store

Running a church is very much like having a retail store. The product you're selling is not a cheap, imported item but is the Gospel of Jesus Christ.

In any retail operation, your focus must remain on your profit, which in the case of the Gospel is not the building of a great cathedral, but the salvation of souls. It's not the amalgamation with another store, another church, or the products off their shelves, but the winning of brand-new souls that have given their lives to the Lord. This is your great commission, the purpose of your whole endeavor.

No matter how big and famous your store becomes, you will go out of business if you are not making a profit. A fancy store may be appealing, but it is your sales that keep you in business.

Many stores go to great expense in advertising and promotions to bring in customers, but if the product that you are selling isn't any good, they will soon leave disappointed with empty shopping bags. While your competitors down the street will advertise that they have lower prices and great deals, you struggle to maintain the quality of your goods, knowing that, in the end, cheap products will not bring lasting or eternal customer satisfaction.

There will always be those who flock to cheaper imported goods because they do not want to pay a higher price, but you know that you must maintain your integrity because of the integrity of what you are selling. It can be dismaying to see the difference between the crowds that flock to Walmart and the trickle that filters in your doors, but you're not competing for price; you are competing for quality.

The cheaper stores do not offer the longevity of quality, the extent of warranty, nor the depth of customer service that you do. Still, you would never win those customers anyway because those customers are only interested in cheap prices for cheap imitations of the real thing. You have won your customers' hearts through the truth, while others have appealed to their customer's parsimony, but your goods are lasting while theirs are transient.

But you still must present something appealing to grow your business. The Bible says that salt is good and that if we lose our savor (or taste), it will do us no good (Luke 14:34). Salt is caustic, and by itself will burn, but food without salt can be bland and tasteless. You can still eat it, but the flavor is gone. So, the gospel must be salted with a mixture of the sharp reproof of the Word of God to bring out the flavor of the Truth.

Salt is also a preservative but must be used in proper amounts. Too much and you will ruin the food; too little and it will lose its savory appeal. The Gospel preserves our souls when salted with that caustic boldness of preaching that can only be generated by a preacher who fears God, not with the bland nature of a weak and insipid message that is afraid of losing their customers.

If the Gospel you preach is unadulterated, pure and strong, and salted with salt, you will win those souls who are not concerned about the price they will have to pay but with the eternal quality of the product you offer.

You will have "customers from Hell', as all retail owners can attest to, but you will also have those satisfied customers who will remain true. Those who will come will be those who are hungry for the Truth. They are not looking for the cheap and easy message of self-focused prosperity and personal blessings. They will be drawn to the symbol that blazons outside your establishment, the Cross that calls them to repentance, and they will kneel down to give their hearts, not their flesh, to Jesus Christ. These are the customers who will remain faithful and true and purchase the product that will last into Eternity.

As for the others, they always have Walmart.

Virgin

Behold, a virgin shall conceive, and bear a son, and shall call his name Immanuel. (Isaiah 7:14)

I have listened to why some modern scholars have chafed at the word "virgin" and replaced it with "young girl" in their newer, more scholastically approved Bible versions. They suggest that another Hebrew word should have been used if it was supposed to mean "virgin." In their typical theological pride, they claim to have better wisdom than the old King James Version archaists. They assure us that we can believe them and rest in their modern laxity because of their educational superiority.

However, with just a little digging, we find that the actual Hebrew word that was used really <u>does</u> mean "virgin," and the alternate word they suggest can only mean "virgin" when it is bolstered by a direct accompanying observation.

Even the Greeks, noted for their exactness, translated it as "virgin" (*parthenos*) in the Septuagint, hundreds of years before Christ ever came. In chapter 1:23, Matthew echoed the same word for "virgin" when he quoted Isaiah. So why, all of a sudden, is there a controversy?

Before the fulfillment of this incredible prophecy, this had to seem like it was an utterly impossible thing to happen. There is no way a virgin can get pregnant, but the old Hebrew and Greek scholars left it as it was written without trying to figure it out.

Ahh, and therein lies the rub! Prophesy is not meant to be figured out; it is meant to be revealed.

Could it be that God created this literary conundrum on purpose to thwart the minds of men? Knowing Man's propensity to rely upon our humanistic endeavors, God had to know that this would create a challenge to faith. Would we trust in our intelligence, or would we cast that away and choose to believe God despite what was seemingly impossible?

The fruit from the Tree of Knowledge of Good and Evil is a fruit that is desired to make one wise, and it has always had a flavor that has attracted the nature of Man. We would rather appear intelligent and figure things out than seem foolish and believe something that defies common sense.

Put in another way, we would rather trust ourselves than trust God.

Today, there is an endless flurry of books written about the puzzling prophesies of the events signaling the end of the world. It has been a treasure trove for publishing houses and notoriety and wealth for the regiments of authors as they bump each other to gain their solitary claim of truth. Let us not forget the readers who, for a mere $19.95, can purchase a piece of fruit that will give them the inside scoop of wisdom.

But as for me, I'm just going to wait and see how God fulfills His word without concocting my own version. I have learned that whenever I try to figure out how God will do something, He always does it in a way I never thought of.

Be careful when exercising your theological analytical wisdom or when listening to those who claim a higher level of understanding. It is all too easy to run down that path in our zeal to learn about God and end up chasing an illusion of wisdom that is plucked off a tree that, while it is beautiful to look upon and seems good to the taste, can be the subtle test between faith and presumption.

And unto man he said, Behold, the fear of the Lord, that is wisdom; and to depart from evil is understanding.

(Job 28:28)

(Quoted from a man who was perfect and upright, and one that feared God, and eschewed evil, and whom God considered one of the top 3 men who ever lived.)

20 Minutes

> *The LORD spake also unto me again, saying, Forasmuch as this people refuseth the waters of Shiloah that go softly, and rejoice in Rezin and Remaliah's son;*
>
> *Now therefore, behold, the Lord bringeth up upon them the waters of the river, strong and many, even the king of Assyria, and all his glory: and he shall come up over all his channels, and go over all his banks:*
>
> *And he shall pass through Judah; he shall overflow and go over, he shall reach even to the neck; and the stretching out of his wings shall fill the breadth of thy land, O Immanuel.*
>
> *(Isaiah 8:5-8)*

Twenty minutes can be a long time when you are desperate, but what about when it is going backward? That was the sign God gave Hezekiah to show him just how much he could trust in the Lord's deliverance.

But that deliverance was not given freely.

The kingdom of Israel had already fully given itself over to idolatry and sin. They used to be the children of God, but they had set up golden calves to worship and had assimilated all the idolatrous ways of the worldly kingdoms around them. They no longer were of the Lord. And now they were going up against the kingdom of Judah to destroy it.

Remaliah's son, the king of Israel, had become confederate with Rezin, the king of Syria, and together they constituted a formidable threat to the safety of Judah. Ahaz, the king of Judah at the time, was scared out of his wits, but instead of trusting in God, he decided to gather up all the riches he could to bribe the Assyrians, another heathen kingdom, to protect him.

God was furious. Ahaz wasn't a good king to begin with, and this just made it worse. He was selling out the people of God in a compromise with a heathen king because he wasn't righteous enough to turn to God himself. He didn't trust God, so he decided to trust the devil.

Whenever you make a deal with the devil, it doesn't last long before it backfires on you. And this one didn't either.

Because of Ahaz's unbelief and his desire to become just like the worldly pagan kingdoms around him, the judgment of God began to roll against His people, "even to the neck" – right up to the very gates of Jerusalem. It wasn't long before Assyria, the very kingdom that Ahaz had bribed, decided to invade Judah during the reign of Ahaz's son, Hezekiah.

But King Hezekiah was made of other stuff.

Faced with extinction by the formidable army of the Assyrians outside the gate, Hezekiah did not turn to some other worldly kingdom to save himself. Instead, he spread his prayers out before the God of Israel in abject humility and repentance, throwing his fate into the hands of God and trusting in His mercy.

It looked bad for the home team. Assyria was gobbling up all the countries around him like a kid eating candy. They had taken all their cities of Judah except for Jerusalem, and now they were outside the walls licking their lips like hungry wolves. But God gave Hezekiah a sign. He would roll back the sun 10 degrees.

I'm not all that smart, but I figure that anybody that can push the sun backward is the One I'm going to trust, and Hezekiah believed the same thing.

As I see the paths that modern Christianity has taken in a downward slide to become more like the worldly religions around them, I wonder if they have become like Ahaz. It's not just their new types of dazzling entertainment and glitz that bother me, but more importantly, it is their compromise of the hard edge of the Gospel with inoffensive messages. While that may give them what they would call "a greater appeal" to sinners, it does not bring repentance – and repentance is what we need.

If we have become more like Ahaz, then can we not expect the same judgment? Even up to the neck?

And when judgment does begin to fall, where will we find leaders like Hezekiah?

It may be that we need to face the specter of extinction with the enemy right outside the gates of Zion to get us to cry out to God for a complete restoration of a church that has forgotten its roots.

Sometimes that's what it takes to get our attention.

The Zeal of Youth

A match is being struck, and a fire is beginning to burn amongst our youth today, and I believe it is the beginning of something great.

This afternoon, I met with a young man that is part of a group that has been holding prayer meetings with other young Christians in their university. They come from different groups and have different backgrounds, but they have found themselves knit together in a strong bond to seek God for revival, and the Lord is answering them.

None of them are established ministers with any degrees in theology, neither do any of them hold a position in any church, nor do they have any agenda that they have been taught to follow – they're just kids who have an insatiable hunger to see God move. They're praying for rain, and it's starting to sprinkle.

Their impromptu prayer meetings are awash with the Spirit of the Lord, and it is fueling their hunger for more. They don't know what to expect, so they're expecting the unexpected. As the intensity of their drive increases, so does the anointing of the Holy Spirit, and the Lord exceeds their expectations every time.

This is how revivals happen. Strong prayer, preceded by repentance and holiness, always brings results. Humility to discard church conventions and allow the Spirit of God to work freely brings a release for a new and fresh anointing that is missing in our traditional view of church. Pastors do not often understand this, but these kids do.

As I listened to his zeal and watched the excitement blaze in his eyes, I thought of David in the wilderness. David has always represented the true church of God, while Saul is a picture of the established church that was once anointed but had fallen away. Saul may have been the king, but David was the one who carried the anointing now.

Although David's group was small in number and considered outlaws, those in Israel who were discontented with the establishment and hungered for the truth flocked to him. This might be a surprise to most traditional Christians, but there are many people today who, just like in David's time, are tired of "church as usual" and are searching for something more. Hardly a week goes by when I do not hear from Christians who are dissatisfied with dead churches and want to find a place that is alive with the Holy Ghost.

They are not satisfied with the stale bread of tradition and the old tales of how things were once upon a time – they want the real thing, and they're not finding it in today's churches. And just like in the times of David, people are hearing about these young people and are coming from all over to get a taste of what God is pouring out.

Revival will not come through the established churches of today, but God is going to raise up stones in their place – stones that are driven with a desperate hunger to see an outpouring of the Holy Ghost like never before and are willing to let God lead the charge.

We may not recognize them because they won't look like what we are accustomed to, and they won't fit our definition of church, but that's okay. They aren't following us; they're following God.

And the LORD shall utter his voice before his army: for his camp is very great: for he is strong that executeth his word.
(Joel 2:11)

Charity

Services out here in Africa are great! You can tell right from the opening prayer that this ain't the U.S.! There's no ceremony, no inhibitions, and no manners when it comes to prayer out here. They pray so hard that you have to wonder if there are extra nails in place to hold the roof on tight.

And then comes the music! They say that white men can't dance, and once you've been in one of these praise and worship services, you will understand the meaning of that saying.

I'm not sure where the transition happens between the music and the Spirit, but somewhere in there, the Lord takes over. Suddenly, you notice that you have this huge grin on your face – so big that it's hurting your cheeks. You're moving back and forth – even stepping to the beat! And the next thing you know, you're out there dancing to the Lord. And you can't stop.

Yeah, the services here are pretty cool. I'm having a lot of fun – even me, a 60-year-old white man who can't dance.

After the message, there is usually a prayer line. If there are any unsaved out there, they are going to get saved. At one service, 30 to 40 souls got saved. They all came in from the surrounding bush to see the Muzungu (white man) and wound up becoming Christians. Pretty cool, huh?

But the prayer line for the people themselves is the thing that is often overwhelming. Sometimes the Spirit of the Lord begins to flow so much that people get, um, "carried away." There have been times when people have been slain in the Spirit just standing in line and even standing in the pews. I'm telling you, stuff happens here that doesn't happen in the States. This is fertile ground for miracles.

The one concern I have is that the miracles would overshadow the message. Money and miracles always catch people's attention and take their focus off the thing that matters most – the Word of God.

Once they see that the Spirit of God is flowing, everybody runs to the altar so they can be touched. These are a needy people, and it is far too easy for them to get lost in their desperate need for a touch from God, but will they forget the greater necessity of what the Lord is trying to impress upon them to bring them to a true revival?

It is the same with the Bibles. Once they hear that Bibles are being given away, people stampede to church to get one. This may seem like a good thing on the surface, but the problem is that we don't have enough money to provide anywhere near the number of Bibles that are needed, never mind enough to satisfy all those who just want a Bible that isn't ragged and falling apart.

Jesus faced this same problem in St. John chapter 6 when they chased him over the Sea of Galilee, not because they heard the Gospel, but because they got a free meal. They get fixated on getting a blessing and miss the message from God that has the power to transform their souls.

There is a message in all this about what we focus on in life. Either we see the world around us in terms of how it relates to us, or we see ourselves in how we relate to others:

One looks for their crown, while the other bears their Cross.

One looks to serve God, while the other looks to be served by God.

One seeks to be blessed; the other seeks to bless.

One consumes, and the other is consumed.

One thinks gain is godliness, while the other thinks godliness is gain.

One of them is going to Heaven.

And now abideth faith, hope, charity, these three; but the greatest of these is charity. (1st Cor. 13:13)

An Abundance of Rain

> *And Elijah said unto Ahab, Get thee up, eat and drink; for there is a sound of abundance of rain. (1 Kings 18:41)*

We are traveling throughout Kenya, visiting a different church in a different city every day. We left Nairobi to preach in Nakuru, came here to Kisii, and tomorrow we will be in Nyamira. This is the way it will be for the next three weeks.

When we first come to a church, we are received warmly but also with a certain amount of trepidation because American preachers have come here before, and the TV is certainly flooded with them, so they have formed an opinion of us as being obsessed with blessings and prosperity. They wonder if I am going to preach that same message. Once they are reassured that the message I am bringing has to do with repentance to bring a revival, they open their doors wide. They instinctively know the difference.

The pastors of the church I was at today had come out of such a deep pit of sin that Americans would have a hard time believing their testimony. The pastor was a hardened criminal, and his wife used to be a witch. The particular type of witchcraft she came out of is so bizarre that, unless all the people around me assured me that these things not only happen in Africa but are common, I would not have believed her. Africa is a very spooky place.

But where sin did abound, Christ did much more abound, and I could feel the difference as soon as I entered their church. This was a place of serious Christians that rang out the praises of God loud enough to pierce the heavens. They weren't there to be entertained or appeased – they wanted to hear the Truth, and they wanted to hear it straight.

Ahhhh. My kind of people.

Now, there are times out here when I start getting worn out and begin to wonder what I'm doing. Am I really having an effect out here? Will there really be a move of God as a result of what I am starting? Or am I just kidding myself with wishful thinking? I don't know if Paul ever went through this stuff on his trips, but the hardest part of the mission can be exhorting yourself to keep driving your message home because God really is going to move.

But today was not such a day.

After driving home a message that challenged them, convicted them, embarrassed them, edified them, and excited them, I brought the service to a close with prayer. Within seconds, I could tell that this was now out of my hands.

The Spirit of God filled the room as the whole church began praying with such strength and conviction that you could have heard them a mile away. When I opened my eyes, I could see people contending with all their might in one corner, others on their knees with their faces on the floor, and others marching back and forth, crying out to God like warriors.

And then it happened.

It was subtle at first but started rolling in like a river. You could see people falling to the floor, overwhelmed by the Spirit of God, while the crescendo and tempo of the prayers increased. We weren't just contending to the Throne of God – we were walking up and down right before God Himself. The Lord had taken over services. It was so intense that I finally just went and sat down – I was done. God was now in control.

This is Africa. I will have more services just like this again and again throughout this trip. It is impossible to describe what this is like to those who are sedate and comfortable back in the U.S. We have nothing like it in a generation or two.

So how do I paint a picture of what it is like in these Holy Ghost-filled services? I don't really know, so I just keep coming out here, preaching my heart out, and watching as the Spirit of God prepares the ground in church after church for a revival in Africa that will burn so hot that we will feel the heat around the world.

The Book of Joel tells us there will be one more revival just before Jesus Christ comes back to Earth, that it will be the greatest revival of all time, and that the Christians will be the strongest Christians that have ever walked the face of the Earth. I believe that I am witnessing the beginnings of that revival.

Elijah said he could hear the sound of an abundance of rain. I can hear the thunder.

Sugar Cane

I am driving through a forest of sugar cane on my way to a church in Bungoma, Kenya to preach a message of revival. There is a sweet, heavy smell that lies in the air as we meander down a mud path that runs alongside fields of 7-foot-high sugar cane. I get this weird feeling of what it would be like to get lost in that jungle with some tiger in there stalking me ... or is that in India?

Anyway, we are off the beaten track way out in the bush, and I am wondering how many people will be waiting at this church. This is not the first time that I preached in a mud hut far out into the bush with only a handful of people in attendance, and in every instance, the Holy Spirit drenches the service. It is almost as if God honors our commitment to preach even to the least of His people in these small, out-of-the-way churches where other big-time preachers will not come.

There is a lot to be said for preaching at small churches. Things happen there that cannot be duplicated in big arenas. Besides the issue of humility and brokenness in extending mercy to the few and the poor, there is something to be said about watching God take a small beginning and use it to magnify His power. Peter was called to a very small meeting in Acts 10, and it opened the door to the dispensation of the Gentiles – no small thing at all.

Regardless of the agenda, I am going to preach there, whether there are a dozen or a hundred. That is if we can find our way through these back roads. As for everything else, I will let God figure it out -- I'm just following His lead.

So far on this trip to Africa, I have preached in over 30 churches. Or maybe that was 40 churches. Everything has become a kaleidoscope of places, churches, pastors, messages, names, and places. Sometimes I wake up with this startling realization that I am halfway around the world, but mostly I just keep marching through a blur of services, aiming for that final date so I can head back home.

As tired as I am, however, it seems like the power of God that falls on each service is greater than the one before – regardless of the size of the congregation. While the message of repentance and revival is just as shattering in each service, the altar calls at the close of service seem to be increasing in power as we go from church to church.

People are touched so deeply that you can feel chains snap and hearts break open like flowers in bloom. Some people seem like they are getting charged as if they have been plugged into an electrical socket as soon as I touch them. Many sway back and forth, floating in a sea of the Spirit as I pray over them, while others simply go into a swoon as soon as the Spirit of God touches them.

You may be thinking that they are just "emotional" and are easily affected by such an intense experience. Listen, I know they aren't faking it because I can feel it as it happens; it's like the Spirit of God flows through me just as they are slain in the Spirit, and I can feel the release of the Holy Ghost as they go down. At the end of each service, I feel like I am a hollow vessel that has had a river pouring through it, and is left empty, washed, and drained. I'm serious – this is as real as it gets!

I'm not entirely sure what is happening in the spiritual realms, but I know that whatever it is, it's increasing in power and intensity as I go from church to church. Whatever it is, we haven't seen this in a long time, and neither have they.

When we finally arrived at the church, it was as I expected – a shed cobbled together with mud walls, dirt floor, and a rusty, corrugated iron roof that was just big enough to hold a couple of dozen people squeezed in together on rickety benches to hear a message from God. And once again, the power of the Holy Ghost poured out in a little tiny spot out in the middle of nowhere to touch the souls of those who were hungry for God.

And I wouldn't want to be anywhere else on the face of the Earth.

Small Places

For who hath despised the day of small things?
(Zechariah 4:10)

God certainly does things His own way. Which is fine with me. I just wish He'd explain to me some of the stuff that He's doing.

I suppose He likes to show us humans how small we are compared to Him. We are easily enamored with our grand illusions and self-importance, but in the face of Eternity, our greatest efforts shrink to insignificance, while even the slightest words that God speaks endures forever.

I guess another reason God keeps us guessing is to teach us to lean on Him instead of on our own understanding. That can mean stepping off the edge of a cliff sometimes, trusting that His hands will be there to catch us. That can stretch your faith to the breaking point sometimes, but the more it stretches, the more it grows. Which is a good thing, of course, but not necessarily a lot of fun.

One of the things that has been a curiosity for me has been the places that He has sent me to preach in. While I would have chosen the biggest churches in town, He has repeatedly sent me to small, out-of-the-way places with poor congregations that would normally be skipped over by larger and more sophisticated evangelists.

While I think that this was a matter of poor planning by the brothers who set things up for me, they have constantly maintained that the Lord set the schedule while they just followed His lead. And they have incredible stories to prove their point.

But the proof is in the pudding, as they say.

A good example is what happened in Bura, Kenya. Don't bother looking for Bura on the map because they don't make the dots that small. Nestled in a valley in view of Mount Kilimanjaro, miles from the main road, is this tiny village that consists of a dozen kiosks in crumbling concrete shelters, with goats and chickens roaming the dirt streets.

Set in this small community is a church and orphanage that we have been asked to preach in for two days. Not only that, but they want three or four services in those two days! There would not be enough time to make it to our meeting in Mombassa, so I had to insist on just two services on Friday. I figured I could split the message of "Four Steps to Revival" between the two services, and I would be done. Everything, however, got turned on its head.

We are out in the middle of nowhere, so I wondered where the people would come from. They filtered in from the bush that surrounds the town, and I walked into a full church that was as alive and ready for something from God as any place that I had been to.

I have learned that mine is not to reason why but just to get up and preach. I will leave the rest up to God and quit trying to figure this stuff out.

The first service was alive and on fire. The second service started with even more intensity, but right toward the end, it was as if I had hit a brick wall and my balloon had lost all its air. What happened? Did I say something wrong? I struggled toward the end, but it was as if someone had turned off the switch!

Just saying the same things that I have said in other places is not enough. It's not a matter of what you say or how you say it. It is a matter of the Holy Spirit that, like a holy wind, carries the message over the pulpit into people's hearts. But it felt like that wind had just died. I felt terrible for these people because they were expecting so much, but I delivered so little. (As if it depended on me.)

Everyone felt it, and they knew exactly what it was. That area is infested with Witch Doctors and other demonic spirits who were determined to stop what God was doing at that meeting, and apparently, they had gone to work casting their spells. I'm talking about the real witchcraft of spells, demons, and black magic. Before you start snickering, let me remind you that Satan is just as real as God is, and one trip to the back roads of Africa will make a quick believer out of you.

It was time for these women to go to work. They told me to get a good night's rest and be ready for the morning. They would be up all night long in battle, and they would get a breakthrough by morning's light.

So much for leaving in the morning for Mombassa. Something big was going on in the Spirit, and I had to see this through.

When I walked into the church Saturday morning, it felt like a fog had passed, and the air was crystal clear. I don't know how else to describe it. The song service was energized, and I felt this thing drop out of Heaven on me while I was singing, "Breakthrough, breakthrough, breakthrough." Whoa, cool!

Once I was on the pulpit, it was like jumping on the back of wild horses. I hung on for dear life and rode like the wind! The Holy Spirit was unfettered, the demonic forces had been broken, and we were in for a ride! I preached the most powerful message that I have ever preached. We were rolling on a wave of the Holy Ghost that took the whole church to spiritual heights that stood us on our feet, waving our hands in the air, shouting and jumping up and down like people who were standing right in front of the Throne of God. There's no describing what it is like when the Spirit of God pours out on a service like that.

What a service!

And the prayer line! Wow! I could feel a river flowing through me as I prayed over each person. The more we prayed, the greater the intensity of the Holy Spirit. The greater the intensity, the more people crowded into the altar to touch the Throne of God. I could barely stand up when it was over and stumbled back to my seat, swaying to the flow of the river of God that had poured out on this little church way out in the bush at a bump in the road called Bura, Kenya. Go figure.

But it doesn't end there. This little church on a dusty road in the middle of the bush has doubled in size from all the souls that have gotten saved since that morning. Already, we are hearing reports that crowds are coming to that little church, and scores of souls are getting saved. This is the same thing that we hear from all over Kenya. Little churches that we have visited have lit up with fire and are spreading that fire all around them.

I would have never picked such an obscure place, but when we throw our reasoning out the window and lean upon Him, we open the door for God to do miracles.

Great things happen in small places.

Wine and Lees

I'm not 100% sure about this, but if I was a betting man, I'd bet that the thing God hates the most is Christian lethargy.

When you have no idea what the Truth is, and you're not all that sure that God exists, you will be attracted to the things in this world because that's what you can see. I understand that; I really do. I don't expect an atheist to be on fire for God – and if he was, I'd figure he was either <u>really</u> crazy or trying to pull some stunt.

I figure God looks at it the same way because He says He would rather you were hot or cold, but if you are lukewarm, He will vomit you out of His mouth. That doesn't leave us much of a choice unless you want to choose the "cold" option, but as near as I can figure, "cold" is going to be rubbing shoulders with "lukewarm" as they both burn in Hell. Maybe the temperature will be a little bit different between the two, I don't know, but I'm not so curious that I want to find out.

Zephaniah put it a different way. He said God was going to destroy those who have not sought the Lord nor inquired for Him (Zeph. 1:6), and he likens it to wine.

I don't know how they do it today, but they used to ferment wine with all the stuffings in it – the grape pulp, skin, seeds, etc. The lees are the sediment that forms during that fermentation, and eventually, the lees settle at the bottom, where they harden.

In other words, these are people that are "in the wine," so to speak. They know about God, have been partakers of the wine of God, and understand and know the Truth, but they are just floating -- Ho hum, La de dah, (yawn) -- slowly drifting down in the bottle, little by little, making their way to the bottom where their lethargy will finally harden their hearts. At that point, they will no longer be part of the wine.

Zephaniah says that these are people that say God will not do good, and neither will He do evil (Zeph. 1:12). They may acknowledge the Truth, but they don't believe in judgment because their God is a God of Love, and He would never exact that kind of terrible judgment on us because He's our Daddy.

Yup. Same lie that Satan told Eve in the Garden of Eden: "Hath God said?" "Oh no, don't worry about that. God wouldn't really kill you." Really? Well, go check for our ancestral couple under "A" for Adam in the phone book and tell me what their address is, will you?

But the real showstopper for me is nestled in Zephaniah 1:12, where God says He will <u>search</u> for these people. He will hunt them! Yikes. It's bad enough to show up at judgment when you are 11 cents short of a dime, but for God to go on the hunt for you? I don't ever want God that mad at me.

So, what is the big deal? Why is being apathetic so bad? What is it that ticks God off so much that He will actually go looking for you to destroy you? After all, most of these people are just good ol' church folks and are really nice people. While they may not be exactly energetic, and I sure wouldn't call them on fire for God, they do go to church. And while they may not be squeaky clean, they don't seem to be <u>that</u> bad. So, what's the problem?

A person who is "settled on his lees" is one who, through spiritual idleness and ease, has gradually become morally indifferent so that sin does not seem so bad anymore. He becomes tolerant of his lack of spiritual drive because he no longer really cares and ultimately becomes hardened to God and sin. In the process, he becomes blind to his spiritual state, and is, in all reality, a Christian Atheist.

But Jesus Christ gave His life on the Cross so souls could be saved. He shed blood for us -- that's how much He cared. When we dismiss the poignancy of that sacrifice and breeze through it as if it was some academic precept, then we find ourselves guilty of trampling the very blood that was shed to save our souls. We will be far more guilty at the Judgment Bar of God than the sinner who never got saved and never understood the reality of Christ's sacrifice. At least they made an honest choice.

While praying one time, I argued, "But God, they're really nice people!"

And His answer came back, "I will spue the lukewarm out of my mouth ... and you think they're <u>nice</u>?"

If they are so nice, why aren't they cut to the heart for lost souls? Or as the prophet put it, "They are not grieved for the affliction of Joseph." (Amos 6:6)

Why are they more infatuated with the world and its prosperity than the sufferings of the Cross?

Why don't they care?

When you allow yourself to be settled on your lees, you begin a separating process that will end with you on the bottom of the bottle, no longer part of the wine of God.

A Sound in the Mulberry Trees

> *And the Philistines came up yet again, and spread themselves in the valley of Rephaim.*
>
> *And when David enquired of the LORD, he said, Thou shalt not go up; but fetch a compass behind them, and come upon them over against the mulberry trees.*
>
> *And let it be, when thou hearest the sound of a going in the tops of the mulberry trees, that then thou shalt bestir thyself: for then shall the LORD go out before thee, to smite the host of the Philistines.*
>
> *(2nd Samuel 5:22-24)*

David was a pretty smart guy. Smart enough to know that he didn't control his destiny. Smart enough to know that life is in the hands of God, and those who ignore that, do so at their peril.

David had just been anointed king over all Israel. He had finally come to the place of his ultimate calling in God, and Satan had gone on full alert. The ears of his minions had picked up at the news of David's ascension, and they knew that if they allowed David to become established on the Throne, it would be devastating for them. They went to war.

The Philistines rushed into battle, probably assuming that they could roll over David's forces. After all, the kingdom had been divided. Many of the troops of Israel had been loyal to Saul's son, Ishbosheth, and had been chasing David for years, but now suddenly, their former employer was dead, and their former enemy was now their boss. David was just now getting settled in Jerusalem, so now was time to strike while he was weak and thrust a stake through Israel's heart.

But they met the Lion of the Tribe of Judah on the battlefield, and it did not go well for them. David was no pushover. He was a warrior of God who zealously pursued the destruction of the enemies of darkness whenever he met them.

Okay, so that was last year. Maybe this year, it would be different.

The Philistines would set up the battle just as before to make David think it would be the same battle that he had won so easily the last time and hope that he would be overconfident and stumble into their trap.

But David feared God.

When a man fears God – <u>really</u> fears Him, not the churchy type of "awesome respect," but the bone-chilling, soul-washing, fear and trembling that the Bible speaks about – then he discards all pretenses to his own ways, his own intelligence, and his own desires. He relies completely upon God for his direction and is afraid to step outside of God's will.

Had David stumbled into the Philistine's trap, he not only might have lost the battle, but he could have destroyed God's Plan of Redemption for the entire world. But David knew that God wasn't just in charge; God was in command. Any victories would have to come through Him and Him alone.

Often, however, in our zeal to pursue what we consider to be our calling to promote the Gospel, we can get ahead of the Lord. We already know what we want to do, so we proceed at full steam, waving the flag of unfettered zeal, but we end up stumbling through the quicksand of our presumption. We confuse what we want to accomplish in God with what God wants to accomplish in us.

We call it pursuing our "vision."

You've heard of that, haven't you? Yup, gotta have a vision! And so, we rush out to manufacture a vision that fits the picture we have in our mind instead of waiting to find out God's vision for us. Rarely are they the same. As it says in Proverbs 20:24, "Man's goings are of the LORD; how can a man then understand his own way?"

When we replace the fear of God with religious zeal, we are destined to fall into the trap that the enemy has set for us.

Wait for the sound of a going in the tops of the mulberry trees.

Child Bearing

> *Notwithstanding she shall be saved in childbearing, if they continue in faith and charity and holiness with sobriety. – (1st Timothy 2:14, 15)*

In the middle of a message I was giving, the Lord showed me that this verse was not referring to women but to the Church. Let's face it, Paul was not saying that if a woman didn't give birth to babies, she was going to Hell, but rather that the purpose of the Body of Christ was to win souls.

If we are the Bride of Christ, then the picture of matrimony is a picture of our relationship with our husband, Jesus Christ. We see, especially in the Old Testament, that it was a shame for a woman to be barren. Besides ministering to her husband, a woman's primary purpose was to bring forth children. Hence Rachael's cry in Genesis 30:1, *"Give me children lest I die!"*

But let's back up a verse or two.

> *For Adam was first formed, then Eve. And Adam was not deceived, but the woman being deceived was in the transgression. (1st Timothy 2:14)*

If we stay with this same analogy, then this is a reference to the fact that Jesus Christ was first before the Church ever was, and Jesus, the first Adam, was sinless, but humanity has fallen and been deceived through sin.

So, then the Church was formed after our Lord, and we are subject to Him. So far, so good. But let's go back a little bit more.

> *Let the woman learn in silence with all subjection. But I suffer not a woman to teach, nor to usurp authority over the man, but to be in silence. (1st Timothy 2:11,12)*

Going back to the actual Greek, we can see that this does not mean that women have to come to church like deaf mutes, but that the words suggest tranquility and proper order in the Church. In other words, don't get crazy on me! Women are to maintain their proper subjection, just as the Church is supposed to remain in subjection to the Lord.

But when we allow our thirst for wisdom to drive us (as in Eve's deception in desiring the Tree of Knowledge), we tend to get ahead of the Lord in our theological pursuits and end up missing the whole point. Never before have we had so many Christian bookstores filled with thousands of Christian self-help books, and yet nowhere in America do we have the powerful moves of God like we had a few generations ago before we were invested with all this Christian scholasticism.

Hmmm. Is something missing? Have we missed the mark someplace? Perhaps we should back off and let the Holy Spirit take over.

Going back just a couple of verses more, we read Paul's admonition to the outward appearance of women in the Church:

In like manner also, that women adorn themselves in modest apparel, with shamefacedness and sobriety; not with broided hair, or gold, or pearls, or costly array; but (which becometh women professing godliness) with good works.
(1st Timothy 2:9,10)

If the analogy holds, then perhaps Paul is not trying to tell women how to dress or wear their makeup. (What man in his right mind would try to tackle something like that?) Maybe it is more of an admonition of how we present our churches.

I have preached in mud huts way out in the jungle where there were only a dozen or so believers and have repeatedly watched the power of God fall so heavily that it crushed people on their faces to the ground, where the Spirit was so strong that you couldn't stop dancing, and where the Shekinah glory beamed so brightly that it overwhelmed you and all you could do is utter praises to God.

Seen that in any of our huge Mega-churches lately?

Constructing huge edifices with golden altars, high-tech sound systems, rich carpets, and laced with opulence and "costly array" to display our "prosperity in the Lord" does not make you holy. Neither does it manifest the power of God. Neither does it win souls. It's a pretty candy wrapper, but it is not the thing that touches God's heart.

The sacrifice that God is looking for comes from your heart, not your outward display. Your wisdom comes from the Word of God, not our vast array of theological knowledge. The focus of Christianity is not about you; it's about others. He wants the sobriety of a church that has the fear of God and is willing to sacrifice all to see souls get saved.

The beginning of 1st Timothy says it well,

"Now the end of the commandment is charity out of a pure heart, and of a good conscience, and of faith unfeigned: From which some having swerved have turned aside unto vain jangling; desiring to be teachers of the law; understanding neither what they say, nor whereof they affirm. (1st Timothy 1:5-7)

Ah, yes. Charity – more important than faith or hope. It is the focus of the Word of God, the essence of Christianity, the purpose of the Cross. Charity transcends all other aspects of the Church because it is the giving of yourself out of love so that souls can be saved. Without it, all we have is Religion.

"She shall be saved in childbearing…"

Crucified Walk Through Suffering

Though He slay me, yet will I trust in Him… (Job 13:15)

Job was a picture of Christ in His sufferings. It is a picture that many Christians try their best to circumvent in their Christian walk, and, as a result, never really understand the path that is set before us as true, converted Christians. But it is the path that takes us to the Cross.

Three universal themes of Christianity come out of this picture: brokenness, suffering, and trust -- all themes that are impossible to fully grasp without a crucified walk in God.

At church the other day, the meaning of a crucified walk was presented as the refusal of sin. But the idea of being crucified with Christ encompasses so much more than that. It is not merely the refusal to allow oneself to fall to temptation, but the severing of our hearts and souls from this world and all its desires, and to reach forth into the realm of God's holiness to walk in His Spirit. There is a change in our point of view that goes from being led by ourselves to surrendering to another master.

Everyone wants to walk in the Spirit, but there is a price to pay for that. It is not accomplished through work or edification; it doesn't come through our efforts, accomplishments, or victories; neither does it reveal itself through seeking wisdom by reading stacks of books. It comes through surrender.

Only when we give up trying to reach God by building our own Tower of Babel and finally acknowledge that, no matter how hard we try, we will never come to that place in God through our own efforts where He, and only He, is in complete and total control of our lives. We read books, do good works, force ourselves to witness, pay money into worthy ministries, and try our hardest to be good Christians worthy of His Love. But all those, while they are wonderful things, will not bring us into the presence of His righteousness. No, you must be broken before God can inhabit you. It will not be by you doing your works, but by allowing Him to do His works in you that opens the door to a crucified walk of total surrender.

To come to that place, you first must admit defeat. Only then can you ever understand the power of the sufferings of the Cross. The world (and worldly Christianity) can never understand that. It is not that we suffer because He suffered first for us, but rather that we are issued into the glory of the Cross by allowing the sufferings of our faith to separate us from this world and all that it has.

The separation of flesh from Spirit opens our eyes to see things in a different light. Becoming a Christian is not like joining some club or becoming a member of some Church, but rather that we now see as God sees because our eyes no longer look through a worldly lens. We are different because we see differently, our desires are no longer our own, and our comfort is no longer our goal.

Once you are broken to that extent, the sufferings of the Body of Christ become the joy of your existence. It no longer matters what happens to you because your life is invested in Him alone. Is there pain? Are there insurmountable problems and destruction that you are going through? Have you lost everything? It no longer matters because you are dead, and your life is hid in Christ (Col. 3:3). You are in that secret place of the Most High (Psalm 91:1), your life is in His hands, and you rest in the knowledge that it is part of His plan for your life.

It takes brokenness to allow us to be willing to suffer for His name's sake.

Whenever I preach, I try to bring forth this one point that encompasses the essence of Salvation: the Gospel of Jesus Christ is not about you; it is about others. Always others. It is the message of the Cross, the cornerstone of Christianity upon which all else is built. Get this wrong, and you will never understand the Cross nor the sufferings of the Body of Christ.

Only once you are broken can you truly trust God. You can trust Him through the valleys, through sickness, through destruction, through the loss of all things, even through death, because it is no longer about you but about the Plan of God. You are broken; your sufferings have extracted you from your fleshly desires, and you are now only an instrument for His glory, and He will direct your paths.

Then you will understand what a crucified walk in God really is.

Three Types of People

For whether is easier, to say, Thy sins be forgiven thee; or to say, Arise, and walk? (Matthew 9:5)

It seems that the people that I meet generally fall into three categories: "really-saved," "think they're saved," or "hungry-saved." This isn't like the five people you will meet in Heaven; this is more like the three people you will meet here on Earth.

True born-again Christians can pop up anywhere. They look like regular guys, so you never know if the person next to you is saved or a sinner, but every once in a while, you will see a face stand out that has a certain look of peace. There's a kind of feeling that surrounds real Christians that makes them stand out in the crowd – it's the Spirit of the Lord, and it speaks louder than words.

A much larger group of people that I meet are those who think for some ungodly reason that if they believe that God is up there, they are going to Heaven. To me, that is the epitome of stupidity. If you're going to blow off something just to twist things to the way that you want them, then choose something other than the thing that will decide your eternal destiny. And yet, so many are cavalier about the only thing that is really important in their lives. Hell burns forever. If you're going to make a mistake in Life, don't make it about Death.

Then there are those people I meet who are starving for the Truth, many of whom attend churches but can't get fed there. I hear that repeatedly, and my heart breaks when listening to these souls who want nothing more than to serve God and to walk in His Spirit but have no strong minister to lead them into the way of strength and power in God. I see in them the futility of a superficial Gospel that has been handed to us by lukewarm ministers. How sad.

The Bible says that the kingdom of God is not in word, but in power (1 Cor. 4:20). It was the power and authority that Jesus spoke with that won souls.

What a difference between a Gospel of words and a Gospel of power! I don't want to just believe – I want to be immersed in the excitement of the moving of the Holy Ghost. I don't just want to know that my sins have been forgiven; I want to walk in power! I want to be like those Christians that you can spot from across the room because of the aura that shines around them from the Spirit of God.

The lady that won my soul was like that. When she would enter a room, you didn't have to know who she was – you just knew that someone who was someone in God had just walked in. She had authority in God – notably missing in our "nice" pastors of today – and a presence that you could feel. It was the anointing of the Holy Ghost.

That kind of presence doesn't come from talking; it comes from fasting, prayer, and long hours on your face before God. Talk, as they say, is cheap. Fasting your guts out and praying your heart out requires a price that human flesh does not want to pay, but that is where power comes from.

Which group do you fall into? Are you one of the lukewarm ones who are sufficed with simply saying, "My sins are forgiven," or are you one of those who want to be able to rise up and walk in the power of Almighty God?

Consider your choice carefully. It will be the decision of your life that will determine your death.

Eagles

> *Remember Lot's wife. (Luke 17:32)*

The Pharisees were at it again. They started needling Jesus about when the end of the world would be. Surely, they were righteous, and this young upstart from Galilee of the Gentiles was no more than a fraud to deceive the people to stray from the established laws of Moses. They were sure that they were bound to catch him in his words sooner or later ... but it kept looking like later and later.

So, Jesus uses the stories of Noah and Lot to describe the suddenness of His Coming. It wasn't that judgment is fickle – it was that the longsuffering of God's mercy has an end, and that end can come in an instant when you are not looking for it.

And then He says, "Remember Lot's wife." Do you remember her story? She followed her husband all the way from the sheepcotes of Abraham, through the division of their herds, and through Lot's fatal decision to move to the fields around Sodom. Through all this, she kept close to her husband.

But it was that last longing for the world that turned her head at the last moment and decided her final destiny.

But she was faithful for so long! Why did mercy fail her at this last moment of indiscretion? Ah, but was it really a last moment of indiscretion, or was it comfortable longing that had nestled in and taken root in her heart and had been dismissed over the years as being insignificant? No big deal. Just a little leaven.

Jesus then relates how that the final division of judgment will cut between even those of the same house, the same laboring of grinding the wheat, even the same fields of harvest – all descriptive analogies of the Church.

"Where will this division be?," they asked.

And His answer is, "Wheresoever the body is, thither will the eagles be gathered together."

I had to ask, what's the deal with the eagles? Well, the word is "aeros," which is translated as "eagles," taking its root meaning from the word "air," describing how eagles fly. While it may be used to describe an eagle, it also brings up an image of "the Prince of the powers of the air," the devil himself.

So, wherever you see the Body of Christ, you will see the devil trying to get in to rip, tear, and divide.

Okay, I understand all that. That's pretty much standard Gospel. But what has that got to do with the Coming of the Lord?

The answer is in verse 33.

Whosoever shall seek to save his life shall lose it; and whosoever shall lose his life shall preserve it. (Luke 17:33)

Some people seek to serve the Lord with all their hearts and are not only willing but pressing to sacrifice the things of this world to serve God. Ask them to give up all their possessions, their hard-earned career, their dreams, and goals that they had for their futures, everything that the world has offered them, and what do they say? Yes! Without hesitation or regret.

But there are others sitting in the same pew, singing the same Gospel songs, professing the same Jesus, grinding the same wheat, and laboring in the same harvest fields. Everything in their lives runs in sync with the Church, and you would hardly see any difference between them and those they are mingled with.

But place them in a position of tribulation, sacrifice, and deep personal subjection, and suddenly their whole perspective changes. Why look for trouble instead of ease? Why not enjoy prosperity and money instead of poverty and self-sacrifice? Why not seek after blessings instead of suffering?

"After all," they say, "since Jesus suffered on the Cross, we shouldn't have to suffer." Uh, that sounds appealing, but it appears you've been skipping over some long passages in your Bible reading ... that is, if you read at all.

The ultimate test of Christianity is not whether you believe that the Gospel is true or not, but whether you will give your life for it – either figuratively or physically.

Yes, you believe in God. Why, you even said a prayer of salvation once upon a time up at the altar! But is your heart crucified with Christ? Does the world hold a tether to your heart that you do not want to give up? Is this reality more important to you than the next? In the end, most people will follow their hearts.

It is easy to be a Christian when life is good, but those pilgrims in this world who look to the Cross for their eternal home hunger for something different. They are willing to go through valleys, take part in the sufferings of Christ, and refuse what this world has to offer to gain that which can only be found at the foot of the Cross.

"These all died in faith, not having received the promises, but having seen them afar off, and were persuaded of them, and embraced them, and confessed that they were strangers and pilgrims on the earth." (Hebrews 11:13)

And that makes all the difference.

Remember Lot's wife.

EULA

Do you know what a EULA agreement is? Have you ever read one?

I have no idea what the E.U.L.A. stands for, but I'm sure I could come up with something appropriate. A EULA is that long multiple-page legal agreement in tiny print that you see whenever you install new software. Remember checking YES and clicking on to the next page?

I never read those things. I can't. And I have tried. I always blow past them in my rush to get finished with whatever installation I was doing. I mean, how bad could it be? What are they going to do? Take my kids? Throw me in jail? I don't have any money, so they can't get that.

And then I began to wonder, just what exactly am I agreeing to? So, I tried reading one. Yeah, you know what that was like. You can't do it – you physically can't do it. Round about the third or fourth paragraph, your mind begins to get weary. You have no idea what you've just read, and you have 90% more to go. You struggle on in a half-hearted attempt to force your way through, but you already know it's hopeless.

It makes me wonder – are lawyers really that smart? Or are they operating in some other dark and diabolical element? (Hey, I don't blame the lawyers. They're just circling around like any good predator that smells food.)

So, what is the point of these EULA's? I am not sure anybody knows, but it seems that it is nothing more than, "Don't blame us if anything goes wrong." If you install their software and it fries your computer, tough -- don't blame them.

What if God was like that?

What if God just tossed us out on the Earth and said, "If you want to breathe, then check the Yes box ... *and don't blame Me if your life turns out rotten!*" In other words, "Good luck. Hope you make it. Don't call Me if you don't."

But thank God, He hasn't done that.

Oh sure, God has a EULA, but it is the opposite of what we would come up with. True, there are some conditions, and it is not a free ticket to ride. God is a God of judgment as much as He is a God of mercy. You can't just check the Yes box and keep blowing on by with life. You'd better read the EULA to find out what you're agreeing to when you check the Yes box. If you check the No box, you already know what you are in for.

But when the hard drive of your life has crashed, when the software that runs your life is corrupted, when there's not enough memory or computing power to go on, then God's EULA says, "Blame Me. Let Me take your sins, your problems, your hard drive failures, and all your corrupted files, and I will make you whole again."

What an incredible deal! God is willing to take our miserable rotten sins, our misery and pain, all our failures and defeats, and trade them for the precious blood of His Son, Jesus Christ. There is no greater deal than that.

Some of us will check the Yes box without ever realizing what the EULA says. Others will refuse the offer, thinking they don't need it, and they will check the No box.

And then there are those who come with broken hearts, corrupted and failed lives, who have given up on the hope of ever being restored in life. It is to those souls who are ready to commit themselves to the mercy of God that His EULA is written to. In checking the Yes box, they give it all to Jesus and agree to the terms of His contract.

The contract and terms of God's agreement are in the Word of God. It is legal and binding, and whether we agree to it or not, Jesus did. He signed it on the bottom line in His own blood and checked the Yes box when He gave His life for us on the Cross.

There is no greater deal written in Eternity.

Neighborhoods

Where I grew up as a kid back East, everyone lived in neighborhoods. The people who lived on your street were almost like an extended family. In a strange way, we were all connected by our neighborhood – it defined us, shaped us, and supported us in ways that exceeded even our families.

I see Life in a similar way. We all live in a City of Life, and we have chosen to reside in certain social neighborhoods within that City. These neighborhoods are defined by their jobs and careers, their moral or immoral values, or by their hobbies and pastimes. Whatever it is in Life that drives our hearts is what determines our social neighborhood. It is not the physical streets of brick and pavement but the avenues of the heart where we really reside, and our neighborhoods are populated by those whose life's pursuits are the same as ours.

Just as in the physical world, there are a lot of reasons why we choose our spiritual neighborhoods. Some of us settle for wherever we live, while most of us move around the City of Life until we find the group we feel most comfortable in. And, of course, there are always the homeless that wander around with no home at all.

Throughout the City are many different precincts that overlap and share streets with other groups, some crisscrossing each other, some running parallel, and others merging for a short distance before diverging from one another. We see each other in the marketplace, waving hello to friends from the Political neighborhood, the Military compound, the Business precinct, and others, but at the end of the day, we always come home to the street that we live on.

The Spiritual neighborhood that I moved to many years ago is unique in that all the streets here point to the ocean. While other neighborhoods are focused on the present, the Spiritual neighborhood looks to an eternal land that lies over the Sea of Death. There are a few distinct major areas in this neighborhood, each with its own main thoroughfares heading to the coast – Christian Blvd, Islam Blvd, Hindu Ave., and a few other less broad streets – but since the seacoast is very irregular, they all point in different directions.

If one was to look at the ocean to which these streets lead, you would see many bridges leading out to sea. Almost all of them extend over the horizon, but there is only one that makes it all the way across to the land on the other side of the ocean. From where you stand on the seashore, you cannot see the other side of this great ocean, so it is hard to see which one of these bridges is the true Bridge. Some people believe that all the bridges will join somewhere out there over the ocean, so it doesn't matter which one you travel on, but most folks believe that theirs is the only one that makes it all the way across. All the others fall short of the eternal life that awaits them on the other side.

Each of these neighborhoods has a myriad of side streets, all claiming to be the best street to lead directly to the true Bridge. Some people have spent a lot of time figuring out why their street is the correct one and offer reams of religious evidence to prove their point. Others just assume that theirs is the best and could care less why.

That would be fine if it wasn't for all the friction that this creates. I have watched a lot of neighborhood rumbles take place, not only between the main Spiritual sections of town, but also between the smaller neighborhoods within each section. Turf wars can be bloody, or they can be calm dissertations of futility, but they all serve one purpose to identify which street you belong to.

Why are they so contentious? Well, one could say that it is because they don't want the others to ignorantly fall off into the ocean by taking a long walk off a short pier. But then why do they get so angry and adamant? Maybe they are just trying to prove to themselves that their neighborhood is the right neighborhood and their street is the best street – or at least it seems that way, especially to folks from other parts of the City who, from a distance, watch these skirmishes (or crusades, depending upon which side you are on).

I saw myself standing under a streetlamp, looking at my roadmap. There are several Maps, one for each neighborhood with several different versions, each claiming to be better than the others. The funny thing is that, even with the same version of the same map, people from different streets go in different directions. I'm not sure if that is a matter of perspective or choice, but it sure can seem confusing if you don't know where you are going.

I'm not sure why they like those other streets. Some of them are very dark like Wicca St., some have artificial fluorescent lighting like Mormon Ave., and others are broad and easy streets that were built a long time ago like Presbyterian Blvd. I suppose that they like the look and feel of their street because it appeals to the desires of their hearts. Some like dark streets so they can hide in the nooks and crannies there, others like to have their own lighting systems that they have made up themselves, while others could care less how bright it is as long as they don't have to change the light bulbs.

I don't know about everyone else, but I chose to live on my particular street in the Christian neighborhood because the streetlights are brighter here, and I can see better on this street than on some of the dark alleyways chosen by some of my neighbors. Mine isn't a broad avenue like some of the others – it is strait and narrow – but it is brightly lit.

There is no doubt in my mind that this street leads directly to that Bridge over the Sea of Death and will ultimately take me to my eternal home. The map I am holding points me in a simple and clear direction, so I don't have to guess as long as I keep that map before me. I can feel the ocean breeze and hear the seagulls. And down at the end of the street, I can see a faint glow of Heaven that filters through the haze on the horizon. As I walk the length of this street, I can smell the scent of Beulah Land that lies just over the horizon.

This is the way, not because I think so, or because my parents settled on this street, or because my friends and neighbors live here, but because I can hear the sound that calls me over the sea to a land that is fairer than day.

By the Brook Cherith

> *And it came to pass, when midday was past, and they prophesied until the time of the offering of the evening sacrifice, that there was neither voice, nor any to answer, nor any that regarded.*
>
> *And Elijah said unto all the people, Come near unto me. And all the people came near unto him. And he repaired the altar of the Lord that was broken down.*
>
> *(1 Kings 18:29,30)*

Just a few years before this showdown on Mount Carmel, Israel had been lush with prosperity and wealth. King Ahab had led the Israelites on a path that led far away from the old, established worship of God that they once followed and had brought them into a life of riches, prosperity, and licentiousness.

The gods that he and his wife Jezebel had enticed the people of God with appealed to their earthly and fleshly desires. No longer did they have to be constricted with an old religion that demanded holiness and the fear of the Lord. No longer did they have to lead a life of separation from the things of the world that other, more prosperous nations enjoyed. They could now enjoy the prosperity and fullness of riches without the constraints of a religion that had become outmoded and old-fashioned.

Life was good. So, when Elijah pronounced the judgments of God upon Israel, they laughed him out of the king's court. The true prophets of God had been eradicated from the public place and were no longer a thorn in the side of everyone who wanted the rewards of love, peace, and prosperity. You were no longer allowed to mention the name of Jehovah, much less pray to him in a public place. They now had priests and prophets of Baal that had replaced those old critical and judgmental men who had caused such consternation in the land.

Elijah had stood as the one, lone voice who cried for a return to righteousness.

And who was this hairy old man? He didn't seem to be of any real consequence. He had no credentials, no theological bearing, and was of no substantial importance. Even his dress revealed his lack of social prominence and his irrelevance in such a modern, sophisticated society as this.

Ahab's ears may have been deaf to Elijah's pronouncement, but when Elijah spoke, God listened. The Ahab's court may have derided him with laughter as he stood before the king, but 3 ½ years later, no one was laughing.

We have followed a course similar to the one that Ahab led Israel down. The Gospel we listen to is far different than the Gospel our grandfathers believed in. We decry the old brush arbor revivalists as hard, judgmental men who did not understand the love of God, and we have traded their message of repentance and holiness for one with a kinder, gentler approach that promises love, peace, and prosperity.

But the love, peace, and prosperity that our modern prophets have promised us are but a worldly shadow of that which God offers us through a walk of righteousness in the fear of the Lord.

We have been like the Israelites at the foot of Mount Sinai – we feared and trembled at the presence of God when the mount shook with fire and smoke, but as soon as Moses departed up the mountain and we were left to our own devices, we made a golden calf for ourselves to worship in God's place.

I believe that something is coming to America that will be far worse than 9/11, but I do not know what form that judgment will take. Would it be a dirty nuclear explosion in one of our cities, or an epidemic, or some natural disaster? In those cases, we would be hurt, but it would not take long to go back to our old ways. We are the great and mighty America, and we have an innate belief that we will always bounce back and dominate.

What if it wasn't any of those imagined disasters but something that struck right to the heart of that which we cherish the most? What if we lost our prosperity and wealth? And what if it consumed every level of our society and every part of our country?

We are living in that time of drought when the ravens fed Elijah by the brook Cherith, right after he fled the king's court.

We look to our televangelists who promise us blessings, and who refuse to consider that our lust for those promises is what has led us to this drought in the first place. But we still flip on the TV and hope for a word of encouragement that will convince us to hang on to a Gospel that has a form of godliness but denies the power thereof. And, of course, our modern prophets tell us precisely what we want to hear, but never a word of reproof or repentance.

The job of a prophet is not to tell you how beloved you are, how many blessings God wants to bestow upon you, or how much love is in your church. The job of a prophet is to rebuild the old broken-down altars of God and declare unto the people of God their sins and transgressions so that they may come to a place of repentance and, once again, return to the true God of Israel.

"Because thou sayest, I am rich, and increased with goods, and have need of nothing; and knowest not that thou art wretched, and miserable, and poor, and blind, and naked:

I counsel thee to buy of me gold tried in the fire, that thou mayest be rich; and white raiment, that thou mayest be clothed, and that the shame of thy nakedness do not appear; and anoint thine eyes with eyesalve, that thou mayest see.

As many as I love, I rebuke and chasten: be zealous therefore, and repent. "

(Revelations 3:17-19)

Three Wise Women

For unto us a child is born, unto us a son is given:
(Isaiah 9:6)

It has been said that if the three wise men at the Nativity had been three wise women, they would have asked directions, arrived on time, cleaned the stable, helped deliver the baby, and given practical gifts.

Of course, had it been one of us men, we would have probably booked a room in the King David Hotel, hired a doctor to be at the bedside, and ordered something off Amazon.com.

I reckon so. But the Lord didn't do it that way, did He?

Why did God decide to bring forth His Savior through common childbirth? Why couldn't He have just stood up in the sky and exposed His Glory for all to see and just told us what to do? That would have dissolved all doubts. That's how we would have done it, wouldn't we?

When the Lord does something, He often moves in ways that the carnal mind would never have chosen. We purchase programs with sets of instructions, plan out campaigns, take surveys, place ads, and pursue anything else that we think will bring about the desired responses. Too often, we end up with something that may look good but does not carry the same eternal weight that it would have had if we had allowed God to do it.

God, on the other hand, chooses foolish things to confound the wise. He calls His prophets out of nowhere, raises up preachers with unpopular messages, and relies on the prayers of people simple enough to believe Him. To bring about His purposes, He uses yielded vessels to carry out His work, not sophisticated intelligent men.

But if it is going to work, it has to be God who does it.

Funny how He works in ways we would never have figured, but you know what? He always gets incredible results. He chose the humblest of births and died the most desecrating of deaths so that we would have the opportunity to choose Him.

Unto us, a child is born. But who would have ever thought that He would have chosen a stable for his birth? But the world has never forgotten it.

And 2,000 years later, wise men still seek Him.

They Sang

> *And the multitude rose up together against them: and the magistrates rent off their clothes, and commanded to beat them. And when they had laid many stripes upon them, they cast them into prison, charging the jailor to keep them safely: Who, having received such a charge, thrust them into the inner prison, and made their feet fast in the stocks.*
>
> *And at midnight Paul and Silas prayed, and sang praises unto God: and the prisoners heard them.*
>
> *(Acts 16:22-25)*

How would you feel if you came into a strange city, excited with a new message of hope for the people there, but just as things are beginning to go well, everything goes wrong? You know that it is the Lord who has brought you here, and you've done exactly what He has told you to do, and yet it seems that, instead of leading to success, it has led to disaster. What happened?

Suddenly, the city has exploded, screaming and yelling all sorts of unfounded accusations against you, none of which are even remotely true. What on earth did you do that was so wrong? You simply shared the Gospel with some of the folks in town when this demon-possessed woman started following you everywhere, mocking you and causing all kinds of trouble. So, when your patience came to an end, you turned and pointed at her and cast out the devils that were in her.

And now all this trouble has fallen upon you, not because you were causing trouble, but merely because this woman's masters were not able to make a buck from her fortune-telling anymore. Excuse me, but did it not occur to them that it was

God who cast out that demon and not Paul? Of course, I don't suppose that matters much when there's money on the line.

So, here's Paul and Silas, not only getting tossed in jail, but beaten to a bloody pulp. Then, to make things worse, they are thrown into the deepest, nastiest part of the dungeon with their feet clamped into wooden stocks.

Did they wonder why God allowed this to happen to them? After all, they had been following what God had told them to do. Was this the price for their obedience? Did God abandon them? Was He busy somewhere else and forgot that they were stuck in prison? Why did God allow this to happen to them?

It was midnight. It had been a long day for these men, and it promised to be a long night. They had no promise of tomorrow and no hope for deliverance. They weren't just tired – they were wasted, beaten, and done in – but they didn't surrender to the exhaustion of their flesh or the cloud of discouragement that Satan tried to blanket them with. No, they grabbed hold of victory by faith, and regardless of the outcome, they lifted their voices to the Heavens and praised the living God.

Can you imagine how tough that must have been? How easy it would have been to succumb to their exhaustion and just roll over and go to sleep. Worry about it in the morning. But they didn't. In the darkness of that dank cell, they held up a light; smothered by a cloud of despair, they held up hope; and in the face of all adversity, they claimed victory. They didn't just pray – they sang! They sang!

And the prisoners heard them.

When I stop and think about that verse, "...and the prisoners heard them," I am encouraged that God sees through all darkness, past the circumstances of our lives, and into the consequences of a faith that reaches far beyond ourselves and places our destiny firmly into the hands of an Almighty God who not only watches over us but has given us the grace to allow Him to use us for His glory.

"They sang ... and the prisoners heard them." I wonder if I could have had that same faith to let the joy of the Holy Ghost flow through me to sing in such a time as that.

But they sang, and an earthquake shook the foundations of that prison and loosed the bands of every prisoner that heard them.

That kind of faith in times of severe adversity, to not only trust God for whatever He has for you, but to sing a song of victory so that all the world can hear that there is nothing that can shake your trust in God, is the kind of faith that makes the earth to shake, that opens prison doors, and that breaks the bonds of those who are imprisoned by sin.

They sang ... and their song is still heard today.

70 Virgins

I have no real personal problems with Muslims ... other than the fact that they are heading for Hell. But that's their problem. If that's what they want, then hey, who am I to stop them? They can believe whatever they choose to believe – just don't try to force me to believe it too.

I'm not saying that we shouldn't witness to them, but we can't force someone to believe what we believe just because we believe it. (Of course, that brings up a whole different message about the necessity to have power in God so that your faith isn't just a bunch of empty words.)

I used to sit in Muslim cafes in Africa and banter back and forth with them, all of us poking fun and arguing with each other. No one ever won those discussions, but of course, there is no telling how much of a residue effect it had on their secret hearts, opening the door for God to deal with them later.

One of the craziest ideas they hold is that if you die a hero for Allah, you get 70 virgins in Heaven. Boy, they like that one! But I believe that is a perfect picture of how misplaced their faith was.

First, you will never get me to believe that God is going to introduce sin into Heaven, no matter how much of a hero you were on Earth. Seventy virgins! What are we thinking here? What, are they just there to wash your feet and cook for you? No, the whole idea is focused on unfettered lust! Do you really think that if you are a good guy, you will be allowed to commit fornication in Eternity? How can that be possible if God is a holy God and hates – literally HATES – sin?

Second, there is no sex in Heaven! Excuse me, but are you planning on dragging your old body of flesh up there so you can cater to it? What on earth would you want to do that for? Are you nuts? I want to get rid of this old thing. Not just to eradicate the old lusts and corrupt passions, but I want to get rid of all these aches and pains. (Believe me, you'll understand when you get to be as old as I am.)

Besides, there is no male or female in Eternity. Ask the angels. Ever heard of them getting married?

But third, who are these virgins, anyway? What, are they bad people assigned to be sex slaves for you? Don't they have souls, also? Or is this their version of Hell, having to cater to your filthy lusts forever and ever?

Of course, this could turn out to be a huge trick on you. Maybe there's a reason why they are still virgins. Maybe they are 80-year-old hags that have been dragged off the streets of Calcutta just to torment you. Wouldn't that be a hoot! Yeah, have fun with that one!

The issue here is not just a conflict of reason but of the incredible weakness of the mind of Man. We are the most adaptable creatures on the face of the Earth and are willing to twist reason to conform to what we want to believe, no matter what the facts are.

Are we, as Christians, any different? Only in degrees.

Human flesh tends to believe what it wants to believe. Why do you think the Israelites at the bottom of Mount Sinai were so quickly and easily swayed to worship a golden calf so soon after seeing God part the Red Sea?

We want to create a God in our own image and are dying to convince ourselves that He will somehow excuse sin – the basis of all heresies. Even the Antichrist, who is as far away from the real Christ as you can get, will deceive even the very elect if possible.

How is that possible? It is possible only when we do not dive into the Word of God and immerse ourselves in deep prevailing prayer to find that secret place of the Most High. We cannot be led by the Spirit of God if we are not making God our dwelling place of habitation. So, in the absence of a walk in the depths of His Word, saturated with prayer, we are left to be dominated by our fleshly desires and, as a result, will be led like sheep to the slaughter.

What a perfect, satanic plan! Make us think we're okay by letting us go to church and mouth the Doxology but keep us from the liberty that can only come from walking in the Spirit of the Lord. Nobody said Satan was stupid.

For the time will come when they will not endure sound doctrine; but after their own lusts shall they heap to themselves teachers, having itching ears;

And they shall turn away their ears from the truth, and shall be turned unto fables.

(2nd Timothy 4:3,4)

Car Salesmen

The other day a friend was saying how much she loved her pastor because "...he doesn't have one judgmental bone in his body." To which I responded, "Well, sometimes that's good...," and then mumbled, "...and sometimes that's not so good."

Stupid me. How many times does Proverbs exhort us to keep our mouths shut? I should have just nodded with "Um-hmm" and left it at that.

In this little discourse is encapsulated the difference between the old-fashioned Gospel and the new Modern Gospel of today. Our perspectives have changed in just a few generations, and we don't even notice it.

We have been told of all kinds of excesses with the old Hellfire and Brimstone preachers, and we use that to justify embracing a kinder, gentler message -- one that is not so "judgmental."

As a result, we have become so afraid of offending anyone that we shrink from warning them about Hell. We are so enamored with a message of love and blessings that we shy away from preaching Holy Ghost conviction to bring anyone to repentance. We eliminate the problem of sin so that now it is more about what God can do for us than what we can do for God.

We have become Used Car Salesmen for God.

Car Salesmen sell the dream, not the vehicle. They will sell you on all the wonderful things this car will do for you, how easy it will make things, how much fun it will be, and how dependable it will prove. You ride away with a picture of yourself driving into the sunset, top-down, hair blowing in the wind.

What they fail to tell you is to make sure you change the oil. If you drive like a reckless maniac, the car is going to break down, and if you don't fix the broken parts, there will be no more riding in the wind. But he doesn't tell you that – he just wants to sell the car.

Mechanics will warn you that there are things you must not do, but you may feel that God is your "Daddy," and, not to worry, Daddy will buy you another car. The truth is that if you don't do what is required to keep the car maintained, you will be in for a long walk.

God has His mechanics, also. They are set as watchmen on the wall to warn us of the approaching danger. If our watchmen do not have the courage to warn us, we are sure to fall prey to sin. Remember, it is not the love of God that causes us to depart from evil but the fear of God (Prov. 16:6).

I hear about love all the time but never about the fear of God. We go on about Heaven, but no one wants to talk about Hell. We want to hear "positive" messages from "feel good" ministries, not "negative" messages of conviction and repentance. We seek wealth and prosperity, but we shun the price of a crucified walk. We want the Crown, not the Cross.

So off we drive, sold by the dream, and ignoring the reality. But it feels so good, doesn't it?

I never want to be part of a church that is afraid of being judgmental. God chastens those whom He loves, without which we are bastards. A wise man loves reproof, the Bible says (Prov. 9:8), but a scorner hates one that reproves him (Prov. 15:12). Paul wrote that it is committed unto us to use spiritual judgment, so yes, judge me, O God, according to your righteousness, so that I may make it into Eternal Life.

I have always said that if God dug a hole on the outskirts of town that went all the way down to Hell so that we could see with our eyes the souls that are screaming in torments, it would change our whole perspective of life and reality. Messages over the pulpits would change overnight. To hell with prosperity! Teach me how to be right with God!

I honestly believe that this is the filter of vanity that God uses to divide the sheep from the goats (Isa. 30:28). He requires us to choose to seek righteousness and the fear of the Lord. But too often, we follow our hearts to a message that leads us like a Pied Piper, to a very different path that leads to a very different destination.

Mary

I have often wondered what it would have been like to have been there when Jesus was crucified. It was the darkest time of the disciple's lives – a time of doubt and despair that they would have to struggle through alone.

They were hunted men – hunted by the very church order that was supposed to worship the same God that they all worshipped. The Sanhedrin had killed the ringleader and would now set about to destroy the rest of Jesus' followers to stamp out forever this new heresy of repentance for the forgiveness of sins. This was not supposed to be the way it ended. There was supposed to be a new kingdom of God on Earth, but now Jesus was dead, and the priests had won.

They couldn't be with him in his last dying moments. As their beloved Master hung in agony, they had to stand afar off to watch while he was surrounded by two dying thieves and some drunken Roman soldiers. Mary stood nearby, but in the end, it was a lawyer and a politician that took his body down, wrapped it in linen and spices, and carried it off to a proper burial tomb.

What a time of introspection! She never understood anything about the death and resurrection of the Messiah, nor did she expect that Jesus would rise from the dead in just a few days. All she knew was that He was dead, she was alone, and it was over. The enemy had won.

Did they ever wonder if it was real, or had it been just a dream? Had they been so enamored with the power of His speech that they had willingly allowed themselves to be carried away with their dreams, or was Jesus really the One spoken about by the prophets? But if he was, then why did God allow him to die and the wicked to triumph? Wasn't it supposed to be the other way around? Aren't the good guys supposed to win, and the wicked be defeated?

And so, the sheep were scattered.

Except for the two Marys. They came as soon as dawn broke.

The task that was before them was gruesome. They had to unwrap the linen, scented with the heavy smell of death and blood, which by now was dried and stuck to his wounds. It would have to be ripped off the wounds, tearing his precious body even more. Every inch of his body would have to be cleansed, anointed, and rewrapped with clean new linen. It was a job only those who truly loved him could endure, because it was not only the body that had died, but the dream, the hope, and the vision of God's deliverance for Israel. The hope of the kingdom of God had died along with him. It was a death beyond death.

Shattered and numb but driven by their devotion, they came early.

There is something unstated about that which touches the very foundation of faith. Joseph and Nicodemus weren't there, even though they had stood in the face of their peers to take him to this tomb when no one else dared. The disciples were in hiding, and how many hundreds of other followers had simply turned back to go home, disillusioned at what seemed to be the ultimate defeat of their hope.

But Mary came early. Jesus was still her Lord. Nothing could change that, not even death.

Faith is unique in that it flourishes in an atmosphere of persecution, grows in soil that is watered with blood, and blooms most brightly in an atmosphere of darkness. Some will answer that it comes by hearing, but in order to hear, your ears must be opened, and that happens in times of stark realities that shatter the soft glow of comfort and pierces the mollified conscience of complacency. It must be tested in persecution to grow and taken to its breaking point to flourish, bloom, and bring forth fruit that will replenish the earth. There is something about the sufferings of the Body of Christ that wins souls.

The challenges Mary faced were like a high wall whose height stretched to the heavens. There was no way to breach it or get around it. Her Lord and Master had been lost to the finality of Death, and it was finished. She knew nothing of theological genealogies or prophetic intricacies. She neither knew about nor would have understood that Jesus would rise from the dead. He was gone, and she was now driven onward, not by any religious understanding or belief, but by a love and devotion that transcended everything else.

It is that kind of love for Truth and righteousness that forms the bedrock upon which faith stands. But as faith rises from that bedrock, it is also bound to the sufferings of the Body of Christ in order to flourish and grow. Only in such a climate do we attain the victory that conquers Death, Hell, and the Grave.

In this darkest time of Mary's life, Jesus was still her Lord. In the face of all adversity, despair, and pain, she held on to the one who had saved her and given her Life. It had finally brought her to the gardener, whose answer forever broke the power of darkness and answered her broken heart when he turned to her and said,

"Mary."

Subjection.

I'm not sure how Webster defines subjection, but I know that there is a very definite meaning in the spiritual realm. But it changes with the times, and that makes it a good indicator of the changing mindset of Christian theology. Today's Christian society leans more on personal independence than unquestioning submission, and as a result, we have lost something in the transition.

Many of us shy away from surrendering too much control to someone else, fearing the excesses we have all seen and read about. And so we should. Those are very real concerns. We are most certainly responsible for the direction of our own lives. So, we lean heavily on the Scripture that tells us to test the spirits and ensure we follow the right path. (Of course, that brings up the question of how we know when it is right and when it only <u>seems</u> right, but that is a whole different message.)

Out of the fear of deception, we set up a set of beliefs in our hearts, and it is against that set of beliefs that we measure everything that we hear from others. If what we hear lines up, then we will follow … as long as that path continues to remain in accord with the guiding precepts we have set up in our hearts. And when it doesn't, we bail out and look for another leader to follow.

That is not subjection. It may sound like it is the right thing to do—and it would be if that leader is not of the Lord -- but as long as we retain a certain measure of control, we have not lent ourselves to total submission. While it is true that we should take advice from others, we take our instructions from God. Nevertheless, God does place us in an army where there are Generals and Captains over us that we are to remain in subjection to regardless of our personal feelings. The trick, of course, is in determining which of those leaders are truly of God. But once we determine that, we are commanded to yield.

Throughout the Word of God, there is a recurring theme of a broken, crucified walk with God that depends on true subjection, not only to the precepts we believe in but also to an unquestioned yielding to the Spirit of God. God does not always lead in the direction we think He should, and neither does He always agree with what we think the Bible says. To know the difference requires the Fear of God – something that has been conveniently left out of our modern theologies and that, as Isaiah 29:13 states, we mention in name only.

Two plus two doesn't always equal four with God, but He requires us to follow the leading of His Spirit anyway. When God leads in a direction that doesn't line up with the precepts we have established in our minds, true subjection will follow anyway. It is part of the process of brokenness that is so necessary to be completely crucified.

It is not an easy process. Brokenness implies pain. But it also gives way to freedom.

God sets up leaders over us – pastors, prophets, apostles, and teachers – but we often make choices that follow our hearts. The subjection that God requires of us, however, leads us to let go of our own ideas, humble ourselves, and submit to those whom He has placed over us. That can be a hard experience for us. The question now becomes whether or not we will submit, or we will rebel and retain our control.

When we refuse to yield to the godly authority that God has placed over us, we are, in effect, setting up our own beliefs as idols. We claim that we have the right to test the spirits, but when we have already been shown the godly authority of the leaders that He has put over us and still rebel, then our perceived humility becomes a form of spiritual pride. When we dismiss the place in God that someone has gained over the years of laboring spent in His fields, the innumerable valleys they have gone through, and the testimony they have built on their knees, then we become scorners. We see from our own limited perspective and do not perceive the greater span of time that gives these leaders a spiritual discernment that we don't understand. Maybe if we would just shut up and listen, we might learn something, but our pride shuts the door of our ears and opens the door of our mouths instead. We become proverbial fools.

To someone who is stubborn and who continually refuses to relinquish their personal control, God often forces that person to submit to leaders who they not only disagree with but may personally dislike. It's as if He is trying one final merciful act to break that controlling spirit within us. And just like a strong-spirited horse, we will either submit to the saddle and reins, or we will be considered useless for God's plan in our lives. You may remain in the barn and be given oats to eat, but God can't use you to the fullness of your calling as long as you retain that little corner in the depths of your heart that you will not let go of.

Ah, but once you let go, you are free. Once you surrender, you win. Once you are broken, He can build you. Once you are yielded, you obtain His strength. Once you give up, He can now take over. And now, God can trust that whichever way He turns the reins, you will follow.

And in that way, all the glory will go to God, not us.

Stampede

In 2002, I stood at the edge of my porch and prayed that God would send another outpouring of the Spirit of God as He had in times past. It had been so long since we had seen real power pour out over the pulpits that no one seemed to remember what it was like.

Many people have come to view church sermons as little more than a religious lecture every Sunday morning – filled with bulleted truths, eloquent ideas, and social advice but stripped of anything supernatural. The pulpit had become the territory of the man behind the pulpit, not a conduit for the power of the Holy Ghost. As a result, we leave our services elevated with religious ideas instead of inspired by the Spirit.

But it was not always so. The revivals of our recent past were filled with fiery displays where the Spirit of God would pour out on everyone there and fill them with the electricity of inspired faith and conviction. Sinners and saints alike could feel the presence of the Holy Spirit, which took them past the words of the message and lifted them in the Spirit. When they left services, they were transformed.

How did things change so much that we no longer realize the difference? And what would it take to bring us back to that place in God that had birthed so many great revivals?

As I continued to pray, I watched as a mass of humanity rumbled before me like a herd of cattle in a mindless stampede. Thousands were running in a mad rush, shoulder to shoulder, not realizing where they were heading but just following the rest of the stampeding crowd. Their eyes seemed blank, only focusing on what was right before them as they rushed along.

A feeling that came across me was that this was Modern Christianity, chasing its dreams of prosperity and good times. It was as if they were hypnotized in a mindless euphoria, with no time for any warnings or anything that interfered with it. It was as if they were locked into it, and nothing could break their trance.

I could see in the distance off to my left that they were heading straight for the edge of a cliff which they would inevitably run over in a mad rush, not understanding the imminent destruction they were heading for. I started to yell and scream at them, trying to warn them, but try as I might, I could not get their attention. Only a few briefly glanced at me before continuing their mad dash into the crowd. I could see a handful of other people way over on the other side of the stampede who were also waving their arms and yelling to them to watch out, but neither did they have any effect.

I was so frustrated that I didn't know what to do. And then I heard the Lord speak quietly to me from over my left shoulder, "Even if they could hear you -- which they can't -- they will not listen."

"But Lord," I cried, "we have to do something!"

It occurred to me at that moment that there were only two ways to stop a stampede. One was to let them run themselves out until they settled down again. But there was not enough time! The cliff was not far away, and they were not slowing down.

The other way was for something explosive to happen to break their hypnotic trance.

"But that has already happened!" I thought as I remembered 9/11.

Then, there was a break to the vision and a sudden stillness began to sink into me along with a realization that something far worse was coming. The tragedy of 9/11 had only been a warning. The repentance and calls to God that we had after 9/11 did not last but a few months or so before we, as a country, went back to our old ways. It shook us, but it did not change us.

As I looked again, it was as if I was seeing the aftermath of a huge explosion that had just occurred. I did not see the explosion, but it was as if an enormous shock had just gone through the air. Dust was settling everywhere, the landscape was barren, and only a handful of people were left stumbling around completely disorientated, as if in shell shock. They remembered that someone had been yelling at them to warn them, but they couldn't remember who.

I watched as one man stumbled up to me and asked, "What should we do?"

"Trust in God!" I answered as loudly as I could so the others could hear. "Trust in God!"

It was then that the Lord spoke once more to me from over my left shoulder, "How will you be able to tell them to trust me, Dale, if you don't trust me." And then, the vision broke.

I know that there will be many people who will believe that I only imagined this because this vision does not fit their view of Christianity or their view of the personality of God. I could spend pages and pages trying to defend this vision, but I have learned over the years that people will believe what they want to believe despite the facts, and they will use the Bible to justify themselves. Or, as the Lord put it to me, even if they could hear – which they can't – they will not listen.

During a broadcast on April 20, 2001, I said that something terrible was coming to shake America. When it came that following September, the Lord reminded me that this is what He had told me about. He also told me we would go into one war after another after another, like an avalanche snowballing down a mountain.

But now, what was this? Something far worse?

There have been prophets that warned us of Katrina, even predicting the correct month it would come, but we dismissed it because we do not believe God would execute that kind of judgment on us.

Then, we had a cataclysmic financial disaster to deal with, and our gods of gold and silver were taken away. But still, few proclaim it to be a result of sin.

I fear that the worst is yet to come. I see in the Bible that God has always uttered His warnings through his prophets, but those warnings are largely ignored. Then God sends a warning that is a precursor for the real thing. The people of God then quickly repent, but after the danger is past, they soon return to their old ways. Judgment was past, and it wasn't so bad, so we are free to once again follow our hearts.

But know assuredly, that when God speaks a judgment, it will surely come – most often when we least expect it. We have heard the warnings, and we have seen the signs, but what is coming will shake Christianity to its very roots.

"The words of wise men are heard in quiet more than the cry of him that ruleth among fools." (Ecclesiastes 9:17)

Untempered Mortar

> ... *one built up a wall, and, lo, others daubed it with untempered morter. (Ezekiel 13:10)*

Two Gospels share the evangelical stage today. Those who have welcomed the new, modern Gospel believe that they have been enlightened by a more sophisticated approach, bolstered by a social psychology that emphasizes a message of reconciliation and positive thinking. We see it in the flow of all the new self-help Christian books and the messages that are poured out from our TV and radio evangelists. We want to feel better about ourselves and shrink from the old, judgmental attitudes of the hellfire and brimstone revivals of the past, so we sway to the music with a "feel good" rhythm that sounds so good to our ears.

Gone are the critical messages that promote the fear of God, the specter of Hell, and judgment for sin. In their place, we have embraced a message of love embellished with promises of blessings. It sounds so good that we feel that it is the one ointment that can soothe what we call "hurting" people.

Those old-fashioned folks who cling to a stricter Gospel are often patronized as, well, ... old-fashioned. Their adherence to an older mindset is considered archaic and ignorant of the newer perspectives of our modern world. "Newer" is translated as "better" and, as a result, more enlightened.

We have incorporated into our religious thinking the spiritual philosophies that have emerged in the last 30 years, primarily from the Oklahoma prophets and promoted by the California televangelists, not realizing that these ideas have not always been the standard.

"Name it and claim it,"

"Seedtime and Harvest,"

"Speak it into existence,"

"Prosperity, love, and blessings,"

"God wants His people to be rich,"

"There will be a great transference of wealth!"

These are all accepted without challenge. They are so accepted that it has become unthinkable that these modern ideas should be challenged or, heaven forbid, could possibly be wrong or at least overstated.

In the face of this push toward a new Gospel, the old-timers feel pressed against the wall of their foundational beliefs. They view this new wave of "love" messages as a one-sided Gospel that ignores the cutting edge of the other side of the Word of God. They don't want to offend anyone needlessly either, but it seems increasingly apparent to them that a softer Gospel is leading to an anemic Church. But to take a strong stand against it only invites ridicule. They are looked upon as old, dried, and hard – old winebottles that are not pliable and forgiving.

Sin has taken on a new set of clothes these days that are more stylish and less condemning.

I have heard one woman praise her pastor, not because he was strong and operated in the power of the Holy Ghost, but because "there is not one judgmental bone in his body."This is the new Gospel – love without judgment. But the Bible tells us that judgment will begin at the house of God.

Proverbs delineate between a fool and a wise man, not by how worried they are of offending someone, but by how they regard reproof. Are we so afraid that we might hurt someone's feelings that we shy away from judging one another by the Word of God? This is exactly what Satan wants. It is a formula for decay that negates God's provision for correction and the strengthening of the Church.

Refusal to submit to godly authority and reproof has given way to a believer's independence. Young Christians often feel righteous in refusing to submit to older authority. Their libraries of modern spirituality books make many feel as if they have a "leg up" on the older Christians who hang on to old-fashioned ideas. They no longer feel the need to subject themselves to any authority that contradicts their own ideas. As a result, they never submit, never listen, and never learn. Instead, *"after their own lusts they heap to themselves teachers, having itching ears"* (2 Timothy 4:3)

This is not new. That same refusal to submit to authority was Satan's downfall. It was the basis for the Temptation in the Garden of Eden and is still seeping into the Church today, eating away at the foundations laid by our forefathers. Paul faced the same problem and warned about it. The prophets that God raised up condemned it, and it is reflected in the fires that shimmered around the golden calf at the foot of Mount Sinai.

No matter how new and modern it may seem, it is as old as the Garden of Eden.

> *Her priests have violated my law, and have profaned mine holy things: they have put no difference between the holy and profane, neither have they showed difference between the unclean and the clean, and have hid their eyes from my sabbaths, and I am profaned among them ...*
>
> *And her prophets have daubed them with untempered morter, seeing vanity, and divining lies unto them, saying, Thus saith the Lord GOD, when the LORD hath not spoken.*
>
> *(Ezekiel 22:26,28)*

Welsh Revival

Much has been said about the Welsh Revival in 1904. It was one of the most unusual moves of God, and it turned the whole idea of church upside down.

It's funny that we call these moves of God "revivals." The incredible supernatural moves of God that we have seen over the centuries are not revivals, because you can't revive a dead body. They are revolutions – revolutions against the established church and secular religion.

Man has a way of organizing things to fit a traditional set of rules. We like rules. I guess they make it easier for us to follow. We construct a box to put our religious concepts into, tie a ribbon on it, and call it Church. The things we can figure out and make sense to us go in the box, and things that do not fit into those organized processes do not.

But it seems God doesn't like boxes. It's too hard for Him to fit in them. So, to show mankind the sovereignty of His ways, He tends to bust up those boxes.

That's the way the Welsh Revival started.

Repeatedly, we have seen that great moves of God are preceded by long periods of intense prayer. The desperation grows like a balloon getting blown up. And then, suddenly, someone will stand up and give a testimony or something seemingly innocuous like that, and bang! The revival takes off like a galloping racehorse, and you cannot stop it.

In Wales, it was a girl who stood up to say that she loved Jesus with all her heart. And the fire fell from Heaven. And kept burning. And burning.

Prayer meetings sprang up everywhere – and not your usual 30-minute polite prayers, but strong, intense all-night battles in prayer. The entire population of Wales was under Holy Ghost conviction, and so many people were getting saved that there was no place to put everyone.

Liquor stores and pubs closed; entire police forces had nothing to do anymore. Even the horses would no longer pull the coal carts into the mines because they were no longer hearing the rough cursing from the miners. Everything shut down.

Church no longer fit in the box.

It has been over a hundred years since the Welsh Revival. We have seen similar moves since then, and all of them fit that same formula, but it's been a while since there has been that kind of incredible, overpowering, revolutionary move of God. But there is one more coming.

Once again, it will not happen as we expect, and neither will it spring up out of the established churches. It will defy the scholastic analyses that flood our Christian Bookstores. God just will not do it our way. He is going to do it His way.

Like watching a balloon being inflated, I can see desperation growing in a place most sophisticated Christians would not expect – Africa. The hunger there is so intense that they will pay any price, overcome any obstacle, and reach to any depth to see God move. Their desire is insatiable. They are desperate for God in the same way that we once were just before revivals broke out in every other place where we have seen God move.

The balloon is growing. As it stretches to the point of bursting, someone, somewhere, will stand up to give a testimony – "I love Jesus with all my heart" – and it will explode. The fire will ignite churches across the land, and it will burn so hot that we will feel the heat around the world.

Out of that fire will come forth a new kind of Christian. They will not be like what you see in your pews. They will not look like what Christians are supposed to look like, they won't sound like them, and they won't act like them. The usual sedate manners that today's churches boast of will be thrown aside in their zeal to proclaim the power of God unto Salvation. They will burn with a fire from off the Altar of God that will consume everything in its path.

You may not like them, but they won't care. They are Joel's Army. And they are coming.

And the LORD shall utter his voice before his army: for his camp is very great: (Joel 2:11)

About the Author

Dalen Garris has been in ministry since the Jesus Movement in California in 1970. In 1997, he began a radio broadcast that ultimately spread to dozens of countries, from Israel and Saudi Arabia to Africa and the Philippines. His program, *Fire in the Hole*, was broadcast for several years across North America on the Sky Angel network as the Voice of Jerusalem.

A newspaper column followed, for which he has written over 700 articles, which have been published in local newspapers and Christian magazines in several countries. He has also written over a dozen books and several booklets.

Since 2004, he has been lighting the fires of revival in churches spread across sub-Saharan Africa. Over the course of 17 years, he has preached in over 1,000 churches and has seen hundreds of them set on fire and explode with growth and hundreds of new ones planted across Africa. Hundreds of people have been supernaturally healed during the healing lines that so often sprang up during these revival meetings, and tens of thousands have been saved.

And the fires are still burning.

Because of his work across Africa, Dalen Garris was awarded an honorary Doctorate in 2017 by the Northwestern Christian University of Florida.

Dr. Garris currently lives with Cindy, his wife of 44 years, in Waxahachie and is still heavily involved with churches across Africa. His pressing hope is in seeing this powerful move of God in Africa ignite us here in America. He believes that this upcoming generation will be the Gideon Generation that will usher in this last, great revival that he has preached about for so many years.

If you would like Dr. Garris to speak at your church or organization, please contact us for times and schedules.

Books by Dalen Garris:

*Available at: **www.Revivalfre.org/books***
Four Steps to Revival
Do You Have Eternal Security?
Standing in the Gap
Two Covenants
Fire in the Hole

Revival Campaigns
The Kenya Diaries
A Trumpet in Nigeria
A Scent of Rain
Into the Heart of Darkness
Fire and Rain
Revival Campaigns in Africa – 2019
The Battle for Nigeria
A Light in the Bush
A Match in Dry Grass
Planting a Seed in Liberia
A Whisper in the Wind
Talking With the Women, by Cindy

A Voice in the Wilderness series:
vol. 1, The Journey Begins
vol. 2, the Early Years
vol. 3, Prophet Rising
vol. 4, Revival in the Wings
vol. 5, Sound of an Abundance of Rain
vol. 6, Watchman, What of the Night?

vol. 7, Mud and Heroes
vol. 8, Ashes in the Morning
vol. 9, Shaking the Olive Tree
vol. 10, Winds of Change
vol. 11, A Final Call
vol. 12, Superficial Shells

Booklets

*Available at: **www.Revivalfire.org/booklets/***

A Volcano in Cape Verde

Tanzania, 2011

Nigeria, 2012

Calvinism Critiqued

When is the Rapture?

RevivalFire Ministries

PO Box 822, Waxahachie, TX 75168

dale@revivalfire.org

www.Revivalfire.org

www.ingramcontent.com/pod-product-compliance
Lightning Source LLC
Chambersburg PA
CBHW031645040426
42453CB00006B/216